SHARING
the
LOAF

Chunks *and* Crumbs
for Our Journey

MARY VICK ROTH

WESTBOW
PRESS®
A DIVISION OF THOMAS NELSON
& ZONDERVAN

WestBow Press books may be ordered through booksellers or by contacting:

WestBow Press
A Division of Thomas Nelson & Zondervan
1663 Liberty Drive
Bloomington, IN 47403
www.westbowpress.com
1 (866) 928-1240

ISBN: 978-1-9736-9690-2 (sc)
ISBN: 978-1-9736-9691-9 (hc)
ISBN: 978-1-9736-9689-6 (e)

Library of Congress Control Number: 2020912990

Print information available on the last page.

WestBow Press rev. date: 09/14/2020

WRITINGS SELECTED BY
SIDNEY L. BRACKMAN CROWCROFT

Mary Vick Roth

Contents

PART 4: MARY'S MUSINGS

Rembrandt Harmenszoon van Rijn, *The Supper at Emmaus*, 1648. Louvre Museum, Paris.

When he broke the bread, it was as if he broke open the whole universe and let light, warmth … hope enter.
When he broke the bread, it was if my stone-cold heart broke open with joy! Ah.

—"Road to Emmaus"

Foreword

Dear Reader,

My friend Mary loved words. She was an avid reader and prolific writer. One year when I opened a birthday card from her, she remarked, "I'm sorry I wrote all over the inside. But you know writers. When we see a blank page, we just have to fill it up." Mary was an excellent teacher, a "natural" as a counselor, and an innovative pastor. We knew each other for twenty-one years, first as pastor and parishioner, then as a friend and partner ("Sharing the Loaf"), and finally as colleagues in the ordained ministry.

I truly believe that of all Mary's gifts, writing was the hallmark of her talents. I met the Reverend Mary Vick Roth in July 1986. She was a new seminary graduate, and her first full-time appointment was as associate pastor of Macomb Wesley United Methodist Church. She and her husband, Merlin, moved into the parsonage on Adams Street in Macomb, Illinois. There was general excitement in the congregation because Mary was our first woman pastor. Especially the women in the congregation were eager to hear the story about her call to the ordained ministry. We soon learned Mary was willing to share her personal journey.

My husband Harry, our three children and I were members of Macomb Wesley United Methodist Church. When Mary arrived, I was working as a school social worker and serving the church in a variety of ministries. I was teaching the junior high Sunday school class, serving as chairperson of the Commission on Church and Society, and participating in United Methodist Women. When Mary left Macomb in 1991 to become a district superintendent, I had decided to say yes to God's call to the ordained ministry.

Mary Evelyn Vick was born on January 30, 1939, in Fort Sill, Oklahoma, the daughter of Kenneth and Evelyn Pilch Vick. On August 25, 1957, she married Merlin Roth in Arcola, Illinois. Mary and Merlin had three children: Marti, Marilyn, and Mark. Their grandchildren include Michael and Patrick Deighan; Sarah, Mary, Hannah, and Leah Kuper; and Siddhartha Roth.

Mary received a bachelor's degree in English and education, a master's degree in guidance and counseling, and a specialist endorsement—all from Eastern Illinois University. She received a master of divinity degree from Garrett-Evangelical Theological Seminary, where she was voted the best preacher in her class in her senior year, 1986.

Mary taught English, speech, and rhetoric at Indianola Junior High School from 1961–1963. From 1963–1979, she taught English, speech, and rhetoric at Jamaica High School in Sidell, Illinois, and served as the drama coach. She was head guidance counselor at South East Fountain School District in Veedersburg, Indiana, from 1979–1981. She had a private practice in counseling and worked with the Department of Corrections, counseling juveniles in alternative placement from 1981–1983. She also worked as a part-time instructor at Eastern Illinois University. In 1981, she answered yes to God's call to the ordained ministry. After successfully completing the *License as a Local Pastor School,* she was appointed as a part-time local pastor at the Batestown United Methodist Church in Batestown, Illinois. Two years later, Mary entered seminary and continued to serve the Batestown Church. She added the Union Corners Church and served both as a student pastor from 1983-1986. Mary served Wesley Church in Macomb from 1986–1991 before being appointed district superintendent of the Springfield District in 1991. She was the second clergywoman to be appointed to the cabinet in the Central Illinois Conference and the first to serve a full and extended term. After one year in Springfield, she was appointed superintendent of the Decatur District, where she served for six years, 1992–1998. She was the first clergywoman to serve as chairperson of the Central Illinois Conference. Following her years as district superintendent, she served the following churches in the Illinois Great Rivers Conference: Normal Calvary, 1998–1999; Quincy Union, 1999–2001; and Knoxville United Methodist, 2001–2005. She retired in 2005.

During her second year at Wesley United Methodist Church, Mary asked me to stay for a few minutes after a church council meeting. She said she wanted to become more involved in the Macomb community by helping to develop and provide needed resources and services for families. She said she knew, that since I was the school social worker for the Macomb School District, I would be on the cutting edge of seeing the needs. I had gotten to know Mary by that time and knew her training and experience as a teacher and counselor would be invaluable for serving in the community.

So, she began her work in the community by facilitating a group for parents who had children diagnosed with attention deficit hyperactivity disorder. The group was sponsored by Parenting Assistance of McDonough County. Parenting Assistance was an education and support agency for parents facing a variety of challenges. Mary soon became a Parenting Assistance board member and worked on the Parenting Assistance's Divorce Mediation Program.

Mary also served on the Positive Youth Development Committee, which awarded grants to various agencies from the Illinois Department of Children and Family Services. Together Mary and I were trained for *Rainbows for All God's Children*. *Rainbows* is a curriculum and method for helping children cope with divorce or the death of a parent. We each facilitated a group of children using that curriculum. We also brought the training program to other professionals in Macomb. Furthermore, Mary served on the Community Aids Education Task Force.

Through working together in the church and in the community, Mary and I sensed that we worked well together. In 1989, she suggested that we form a partnership, and after some discussion, we decided to call it "Sharing the Loaf." Because Jesus is the bread of life, we are sharing the loaf when we share the love and compassion of Jesus with others. Our first project was to write a study guide for the novel *Joshua* by Joseph Girzone. The guide was used by the adult and junior and senior high school Sunday school classes at Macomb Wesley United Methodist Church. Next, we received requests to lead spiritual formation retreats for women's groups. We led six retreats, got positive evaluations, and began to discern that this was an area to which God had called us. Our hope was to continue this ministry in retirement. Mary shared with me her dream of writing a book, "the great American novel." Her writing ability had caught the attention of several of her professors and fellow-students at Garrett-Evangelical Seminary. They encouraged her to keep writing.

Unfortunately, Mary's retirement was plagued with poor health, so her novel wasn't written. After her death on April 14, 2008, I began to think about how her writings could be shared. With Merlin's help, I have compiled this book with a variety of her writings. The preparation of this book for publication has been a demanding but satisfying accomplishment. I am forever thankful for the assistance and advise of my good friends, Katrin Bosch and Valerie Vlahakis. The tireless effort of our granddaughter, Grace Crowcroft with typing, reading, making corrections and formatting is greatly appreciated. Thank you to the Reverend Paul Unger, retired United Methodist pastor for his endorsement of the book. I am deeply grateful to my husband, Harry G. Crowcroft for his loving support of my work on the book. I also want to thank and express my appreciation to the persons at WestBow Press who guided me through the publishing process with great skill and patience. Royalties earned from the sale of this book will go to the scholarship fund at Garrett-Evangelical Theological Seminary. So read, reflect, and enjoy.

Shalom,
Sidney L. Brackman Crowcroft

PS: Merlin Roth, Mary's husband, died on December 7, 2019. Katrin Bosch died May 30, 2020.

PART 1

Memoirs

1

A Spiritual Autobiography

But human beings are born to trouble
just as the sparks fly upward.
—Job 5:7 (NRSV)

Voices of farmers who came to town for Saturday night blended into quiet cadences occasionally punctuated by laughter and mingling with the odors of new leather shoes and rubber goulashes, of dust and new clothes. My ear was caught by a nearby conversation, just above the table under which I had crept as usual after the movie to await closing time. The intense, confidential tone of my aunt's familiar rasping voice separated these words from the background drone as I listened where I lurked: "The baby killed her. Heart, you know. The doctor said she should never have had any children. There was damage from rheumatic fever. She lived until Mary was two. Then her heart just gave out."

I sat stunned, my comic book and candy bar forgotten. No wonder Daddy had seemed so mad at me. No wonder the stepmother who had come later physically and verbally abused me! No wonder my uncle and cousins had mocked and teased me! I had killed the beautiful woman who was my mother. I had destroyed the lady whom Nana had already canonized a saint along with Grandfather.

In that moment under the large merchandise table in the dry goods store, I learned that I was a murderer, and I began to believe that I deserved the secondary status the world afforded me. From the moment of that fragment of conversation, I began to filter everything that had and would happen to me through the assumption that I was bad, maybe evil.

I came to understand why I had moved around from relative to relative from the time my mother died. From two years of age, when I had murdered my mother, I had stayed in one place for only short periods. No wonder!

Only Nana didn't fit the picture. Mother's mother loved me. She, who told such loving, exciting stories of my mother, loved even me. If God existed in those days, God was four feet, eleven inches tall and spoke with a thick Middle-European accent.

Nana didn't fit. Her unconditional love almost persuaded me, who wanted so badly to believe that I was loved, that I had some worth. Nana took me to her big city church, built of red brick with stained-glass windows. I clutched her hand as I passed among the dour-faced widows and spinsters, their mouths were pursed into invisibility by their piety. I asked, "Why are they mad?"

"Shh," Nana whispered. "They are saints. They are good women." Sitting beside Nana on the hard oak pew, short legs swinging only a little above the floor, I prayed earnestly, "God, don't make me so holy my lips disappear. Amen."

When I was not fortunate enough to escape the terror of the farm to spend weekends with Nana, I attended the white clapboard church on the hill down the road. There folks gathered from the surrounding farms for a weekly social event. There my cousins continued their persecution, and I could not escape into invisibility. There the preacher lamented the congregation's sinfulness in such scathing tones that I was certain that he could see right into my murderous heart. There God wore a judgmental scowl and lurked in wait for an excuse to strike me dead with lightning-bolt words.

Except for escapes to Nana's loving arms and occasional letters from a father almost forgotten, life was almost unbearable … until I learned to read. Studying my cousins' abandoned primers, driven by curiosity, I badgered my aunt with questions until I learned to read—and to escape! I existed in other worlds, exciting and adventure-filled worlds between the covers of books. I left them only under dire threats from my aunt or to worry the piano keys with my sad songs. Then Nana died and we moved to town, although without the piano, which had become one source of release for me.

There was no room for my piano, but the family grudgingly made room for me. I had been taught by that time that I was worthless and deserved nothing. I was supposed to be grateful for shelter and care. I learned instead to be resentful, feeling helpless to demand more than crumbs lest even those be taken away. I was silent and secretive enduring my lot, except on the many occasions when I tried to run away. I did not learn to give and receive love. I refused for many, many years to learn to be grateful. Instead, I learned about duty and guilt and self-contempt.

A woman in the neighborhood became friends with my aunt, and I adopted her. Her beauty, her gentle voice, her rippling laugh, and attentiveness made Norma the mother I so much wanted. But my jealous aunt forbade my visits, and I saw less and less of Norma. I was adopted instead by a classmate whose schoolteacher mother and school principal father encouraged me to do well in school. I began a pendulum swing from happy, carefree times at Judy's home—encouraged and valued, playing the piano I had so sorely missed—to strange, tense evenings when I was called to spend the evening with Norma when her husband had to work. I had liked being with this kind and beautiful woman, but times with her grew increasingly frightening. Whatever furies haunted her drew very near at times. I sensed as we sat in her warm kitchen that she saw things unseen by me, more vividly than objects actually in the room.

No one told me Norma was a cyclic depressive whose periodic psychotic breaks were becoming so severe that my aunt feared she would kill herself. She only said, "Norma wants you to come over and stay with her tonight."

One night I didn't go. An invitation to go to Judy's to play the piano and do homework promised a pleasanter evening. My aunt's plea that "You're the only one who can help her when she is like this" was ignored. The next morning at dawn, Norma poured gasoline over herself and struck a match. As the wail of the ambulance faded into the distance, I knew that once more I was a murderer. I carried the new shame with me silently, seeking to somehow make up for the terrible things I had done. I worked hard in school, drawn to becoming something. My father invited me to spend the summer with him, and I was overjoyed to be wanted, but when he came bringing my stepmother and stepsister, I could hardly control my fear. The repeated jealous attacks terrified me, and when my father informed me that he expected me to stay past summer, I refused to go at all. I learned then not to trust anyone and not to expect to be loved.

Becoming best friends with the new pastor's daughter, I went back to the church I had attended with Nana. I confessed my sins to God and felt forgiveness. I became president of the Methodist Youth Fellowship. When I was fifteen, I attended an M.Y.F. meeting in Springfield, Illinois, where a dynamic young speaker commanded, "Spend your life for something that will outlast it." I heard the echoes years later.

A local doctor had encouraged me when I expressed an interest in medical school. An uncle agreed to foot the bills. My drive to become educated and to serve was intensified when three of the four boys I had dated suffered tragic accidents. One was disfigured. Two were paralyzed from the neck down, one later dying from pneumonia.

I sat in Mr. Long's English class that warm autumn afternoon, lulled by the heat and flies droning. We struggled to remain awake through scene after scene of Macbeth's witches. As he explained the meaning of the storm, the signs and portents, omens of evil to come, I began to tremble. When Lady Macbeth wept in her somnambulistic moan, "What, will these hands ne'er be clean!" I felt accursed, stalked by death, a living, breathing Typhoid Mary, bringing tragedy to those I touched. I would, at that moment of adolescent frenzy, never love again, never become close to anyone again. People I grew close to had died, as had the doctor who had encouraged my longing to go to medical school.

Weeks before my graduation from high school, my uncle suggested that I didn't need a college education to have babies. Since this was not my career goal, I sought other financial assistance. I refused to ask my father for a copy of his discharge papers to obtain a scholarship. I had not communicated with him for four years. I did not want his help. I would depend on no one.

When the University of Illinois insisted that I must enroll as an out-of-state student, I used two teacher education scholarships that I had managed to earn and went to Eastern Illinois University the summer following my high school graduation. I was proud of my straight-A high school record, proud of my strength. I lived from the neck up, alone, silent, except for the bad poetry I wrote, self-sufficient and scared.

Nobody in my family had ever been to college. I wasn't sure I could survive. I was alone, afraid, and suddenly wanting very much to be loved and cared for. I don't know how I overcame my fear that anyone I came to love I would destroy, but I married at eighteen. I wanted to be loved, yet did not know how to give or receive it. I wanted a home yet felt too driven to excel in school to spend time on much else. Odd that I gave up the "different" identity I treasured and became like my aunt and cousin—a housewife.

My self-concept depended entirely upon my grades. The only praise or rewards I had ever received were the results of my academic efforts. If I failed there, I was a total failure.

An unplanned addition to our family interrupted my college work and cost me my scholarships. So it was only after nine years of intermittent enrollment that I was able to complete work toward a bachelor's degree. My college work was a mixture of brilliance and mediocrity, the former when challenging teachers inspired me, the latter with the news that the third child I was carrying would be born mentally challenged with a cleft palate because of medication I had been taking before I knew I was pregnant.

Long months of guilt, shame, terror, and self-blame eased when an apparently normal child was born. Soon, however, we realized that our son wasn't normal. He had a near-genius IQ and mild learning disabilities due to minimal brain damage. The seven years I worked with him and found competent professionals who found what was wrong and how to compensate drew us very close.

I became a good teacher. But as increasingly numbers of hurting, lost students turned to me for help, I decided my natural skills as a counselor needed to be enhanced by training. I returned to school for a master's degree in counseling.

In addition, I gained self-understanding and for the first time a real understanding of God's love. The teachers were Carl Rodgers and a professor named Bob. I came to understand by reading *On Becoming a Person* and studying with Bob about unconditional love. Psychology almost became my religion as I saw the gospel of love lived out more fully than I had ever been able to recognize it in church people. I began to love, feel, enjoy life, and give myself permission to play.

About this time, a wonderful pastor came into our lives. After a long separation, God and I got back together. We had both changed. God was more convincingly forgiving yet more demanding. I had learned to harness my anger. Instead of pitying myself for the tragedies in my life, I had become Prometheus, one who brings the light of truth, the fire of commitment to people. As a teacher, I wanted to inspire others with the messages I had learned, including this one: spend your life for something that will outlast it. I knew before I'd ever heard of Viktor Frankl that those who had survived the Holocaust were those who lived for others.

Had it not been for Paul Unger, I might have strayed from the church completely. Paul was a powerful preacher who gave me new images of God and a contemporary interpretation of what it meant to be a disciple of Jesus Christ. Paul asked hard questions instead of giving pat answers. The familiar "Road Not Taken" preaching began to speak to me for the first time.

I came to know that God loves me. And I began to forgive myself. The anger, fear, and self-contempt that had driven me began to ease. I became freer to care for others. Even before I completed my counselor's training, I was counseling Patty, whose long-distance calls lasted for hours when she was most depressed. She didn't kill herself. Hers was the first wedding at which I assisted. I saw in her rebelliousness against the church memories of my own earlier condemnation of its imperfections. I heard John B.'s rage and pain after the preacher at his father's funeral began his message with, "Mr. B. was not a Christian; he is in hell."

These and other students taught me how to minister. But for seven years, I ministered as a counselor. I sought to help students or juvenile offenders achieve self-understanding and wholeness; to learn to cope with a broken, hurting world; to find meaning and purpose in their lives. I worked to acquire another degree. My dissertation was the development of a holistic counseling model. Through the work, I sharpened my skills as a therapist and came to a better understanding of the whole self.

The final absolution of childhood guilt and ghosts came with my father. I came to understand that he, whose parents had died when he was six years old, had difficulty giving and receiving love. I realized he wasn't to blame for much of what had happened to me and that he had done the best he was capable of doing as a parent.

In this long pilgrim melody, I have found grace notes and discords giving me positive and negative images of ministers. Above all, I have found God, who was there all the time though I knew him not. And I have found a new song to sing.

God began calling me a long time ago. I didn't listen clearly. The stories of Grandfather, a clergyman in the Central Illinois Conference, were part of my earliest memories but were far removed from anything I had heard God saying to me.

My answer to the call was to teach Sunday school and spend hours in arguments with the pastor next door. I wrote dramas for youth groups to perform at Christmas and evaded any comments from God about any deeper involvement.

My ministries were my teaching and counseling. After all, weren't these the gifts God had given me? As early as junior high, I was the one with the ready ear to hear my peers' problems; my shoulder had been wet since grade six. My favorite counseling professor called me "a natural," and I taught more than I learned in graduate school. What more could God ask than that I develop and use the gifts the Lord had given me?

If she hadn't been such a good friend, I'd have fought longer. But Sandy was persistent, urging me to teach at the School of Christian Mission. I'd never been to one; I'd avoided the United Methodist Women (UMW) like the plague. I had my work. But God kept calling, and I had trouble saying no to new adventures.

To be certified to teach, I had to read a number of books and attend a regional school in Sioux City. Lindsey Pheriga's class and conversations after class began to stir me; my roommate's assumption that I, too, was an ordained clergywoman startled me. Women can be clergy? What are you getting at, God? Leave me alone.

I taught at the School of Christian Mission, terrified that the women there, my students, would find out how little I was and knew. I went back to my counseling job "dis-eased," troubled that God and I were in for a long argument about my future. I bought time teaching a difficult church school class and counseling with troubled persons in the congregation. I began to feel that I had found my ministry until the insecurities of my home church made my situation untenable.

I decided that if I couldn't use my gifts in my home church, I'd return to school for my doctor's degree and set up my own Christian counseling center. I'd been taking private cases for a number of years and looked forward to working in a context in which I could openly minister to the whole person, dealing with both spiritual and emotional needs, which I couldn't do in the public school setting.

I was running away from God's call into the ordained ministry. I kept hoping but not believing. I was hearing the call wrong. I don't even remember now why I ran from it. Too awe-filled I think.

On February 14, 1980, I had the most perfect day of my life. I had a number of breakthroughs in therapy, a Valentine's Day dinner date with my husband, a concert at the university, and a leisurely drive home while discussing our futures.

On February 15, 1980, God yelled at me. A number of coincidences, which only hindsight disclosed, should have warned me. But I wasn't watching that night as I returned home from work. A sudden icing up of a steeply banked curve threw my little car into the largest Ford I had ever seen.

As I drifted in and out of consciousness, I thanked God that for the first time in two years, my husband hadn't shared the ride home from work. As the rescue workers struggled to release my knees and feet from the crumpled car that ensnared them, I had only a strong sensation of the presence of God with me. The doctor who sewed my face back together was wonderful, and when I awoke in a hospital bed, the crucifix on the wall facing my bed told me why I was there.

I had already learned to see the cross as a great big "I" with a minus sign through it. With my concussion, the cross before me often appeared to have two cross bars. I got the message: subtract more of the "I." Forget my dreams and answer God's call.

I entered the candidacy process, and following an interview by the District Board of Ordained Ministry in March 1981, I was offered an appointment. I attended the school for local pastors and was installed in my first appointment in July 1981.

Because we had two children in college, I decided to delay entering seminary and continued in my professional job to pay the bills while pastoring evenings and weekends. I struggled with guilt over the delay, hoping God would understand that I hadn't put my hand to the plow and turned back.

I struggled, too, to take the final leap of faith to give up everything: professional status, having just earned the respect of a difficult boss and worked up to a powerful, challenging, and exciting position. But to give up everything was the call. Only when I had nothing could I have everything.

I was careful and thoughtful in my search for the right seminary. I wanted to choose for the right reasons. I visited several in various parts of the country. I chose Garrett because when I sat down there and mentioned those coincidences with a smile, five knowing smiles in five nodding faces signaled, *Yes, we know. Welcome home.*

I was so certain God was calling me to specialize in pastoral care in some capacity that I was totally surprised to be called, for the present at least, into local parish ministry. Life was good for me there.

My understandings of ministry come from three independent sources impacting and informing one another. First are my readings, bits and pieces that have caught my consciousness from time to time. Second are from experiences where I or others were ministered to, out of which come great affirmations and denials of what ministry is and is not. Third are from my nearly three years as local church pastor.

Henri Nouwen says that ministry is hearing the pain of the other, having the courage to enter where life is experienced as most unique and most private, where one touches the soul of the community. That is the "ministry of presence" in which I was engaged for so long before I had a label for it. It meant being with others in the depths of where they most truly are, standing with them and giving not advice but one's self.[1]

For me ministry is using one's gifts in such a way that others come to develop and use their gifts to praise and serve God. Ministry is loving persons as they are so they may become what God meant them to be. This means helping one another to find wholeness in a fragmented world. We do this by gaining the insight and courage to reclaim pieces of ourselves. The healings Jesus did were exemplary, serving as signs of who God is. Being in ministry means being called by God, as all Christians are, to heal, to teach, to proclaim the gospel, to free the oppressed, and to feed the hungry, whether or not they are set apart as priest. It means being either someone seen as a mediator between God and people and therefore being set apart from the people and taking on the attributes of God. Or it means being seen as pastor, servant, or one who is deeply for, with, and among the people.

I believe ministry is helping persons achieve a balance among those parts of themselves the world acts like are separable parts, discrete entities. Ministry, I believe, is more than any of its components. To minister is to preach the word, to administer the sacraments, to pastor, to teach, to administer the resources of the church, to attack oppressive social systems, to build up and edify the body, and to be in mission and so forth. Ministry is afflicting the comfortable while comforting the afflicted. To be in ministry is to preach the word by one's life and one's word. One's greatest contribution to the work of the kingdom should be one's self.

I believe ministry is servanthood, stripping oneself naked before God and humanity, and washing others' feet. I learned servanthood early. I learned that to be forced into the servant role breeds resentful submission. Fortunately, I also learned that to serve as a spontaneous outpouring of love in response to being loved is a source of great joy.

I believe ministry is interpreting the ways of God to men. It is not being too late. A loud knocking on the front door awakened me at about three o'clock in the morning. I was wanted at the hospital. Bill had been taken to the emergency room, probably a heart attack. His wife was calling for me. *Dress, grab my Bible, hurry.* Would I be too late? As my car hastened across town, I remembered the death of Bill's best friend, Howard. It had been a long dying, as laborious as a birthing as the strong heart sought to keep a cancer-ridden body alive. There was time to share, to talk out the grieving, the questioning, the raging, the doubting. My car, blessed by the "clergy" sticker, slipped into the no-parking zone, and I hastened to the emergency room. The wailing of newly widowed Barb soared on shrill obbligatos above her sister's quiet chant, "God's will … God's will …" Beside Barb, her son's eyes, black with rage, sought my face. Was I too late?

I wasn't too late … except for Stevie. I can still see the rage in his black eyes at the visitation. "It's God's will now. Your grandpa is with God, son. God wanted Grandpa with him, so he took him to be with him in heaven." Twelve-year-old eyes stared into mine for confirmation or denial. A walk, a talk, a listen, so accepting of the poured-out rage, and then peace. I hadn't been too late after all.

I believe that to minster is to help persons wrestle with those most difficult questions of human existence and find their own answers.*

---

* Mary's autobiographical essay is an edited version of her paper for the Introduction to Ministry class at Garrett-Evangelical Theological Seminary.

2

The Turquoise Dress

I walked a little faster, hoping my cousins would lose interest in teasing me. But their taunts just became louder. It was hard to walk fast anyway with my hand-me-down taffeta dress in that horribly loud emerald green color swishing noisily. Soon I reached the steps of the white-framed church and dashed inside, almost tripping into an elderly parishioner.

"'Scuse me," I mumbled as I darted by.

"Lord, have mercy!" she croaked, shaking her head.

I hurried to the pew where my family always sat and scooted to the very end of the dark-varnished pew. My bare thigh squeaked on the wood, made sticky by heat and humidity. I squirmed into a prim posture and bowed my head. My cousins, still snickering, bumped into the pew beside me.

Soon the piano pounded out a familiar gospel tune, and the congregation rose to wail out "Amazing Grace."

When we were seated, the minister began. His voice grew stronger as he neared the main point of his sermon. I looked up just as he shouted, "God loves you!" Perhaps it was my sudden movement that caught his eye and distracted him. Perhaps it was God's doing. At any rate, he looked intently at me as he repeated the words, louder still. "God loves *you*!"

Startled, I stared at him as if I'd never before seen his red and sweating face looming over the pulpit. He seemed like God himself speaking to me.

As soon as the singing of the last hymn died away, I lurched up the side aisle, raced down the steps, and scampered along the dirt road as quickly as I could run. This time it was wonder rather than shame that propelled me. I ran and ran until I could dash onto the porch of our farmhouse.

The screen door thudded behind me as I puffed up the stairs and paused, panting in the doorway of my room.

I shut the door carefully behind me, sat on the edge of my bed, and carefully removed my black patent shoes. Then I knelt beside my bed, as if on holy ground, and whispered, "God, it's me, Mary. I love you, too."

3

Nana's Coming

Winter was the worst, for then the world seemed always dark. The gloom of the paneled breakfast nook was relieved only briefly at midday. The dining room always lay in darkness. Musty smelling, it was populated by dark chairs and table with complicated legs and ornate carvings.

It was my job to dust them. And I was afraid. I don't remember what I feared lurked in the room's shadows, but I do remember the fear.

I was given the smelly dust cloth and ordered to go and dust. The task seemed endless, and sometimes my fear changed to terror before I could finish. I couldn't hurry by skipping any of the rungs or intricately carved details, for if caught, I would be ordered to begin again, and by then I would be nearly paralyzed with fear.

I don't recall ever questioning the necessity of dusting the unused furniture in an unused room. There were many demands put on me, which I didn't question or resist. Winter was the worst but only by a little.

Summers were the season of going to bed at the usual hour of eight o'clock, no matter that oppressive heat pressed me down against the white sheet while rivulets of perspiration and tears ran into my ears. No matter that the laughter of neighbor children catching lightning bugs reached me where I lay. No matter. No matter that my stepsister, younger than I, was cooed over, played over, and admired in the living room. No matter. Eight o'clock was the time, and I went to bed.

Once when the sultry air seemed particularly oppressive, I sought relief by sticking my feet on the windowsill, hopeful that a wisp of breeze might cool them.

I was discovered. A frenzy of shouting, slaps, and chastisement followed.

If I were fortunate, I might be tired enough that the squeak of the porch swing or murmurs of neighbors chatting might lull me to sleep.

One memorable night, I heard heavy footsteps, and my father entered my room. He greeted me in his too-cheerful tone that he used when he pretended everything was fine. My stomach tensed. I wanted to go to the bathroom with sudden urgency.

"Let's go out on the porch," my father invited, lifting me from the bed. He set me down in the swing and sat beside me. Fireflies worked in the dusk. The bright flowers of the scarlet runner beams were graying as darkness fell. I reached out to touch the nearest vine. The velvety leaves brushed my fingers as the porch swing eased forward.

"The vines will have flowers on them later," Daddy remarked. His voice was softer now.

"I won't be here to see them. I'm going away," I answered.

The swing stopped with a sharp creak. "How did you know? Who told you? Did ...?"

Daddy grabbed me with his strong hands. His voice was getting louder. I froze. He kept shaking me, then stopped suddenly. I fell back against the swing when he let me go. Neither of us moved. "You must have heard us talking," he said.

I was silent.

"You'll be leaving next week. Nana is coming to get you."

More silence. I was very still, feeling some relief that the words I had guessed were coming had been spoken. I was careful to show none of the joy I'd been holding back for so long while I had only unconfirmed hope that I was escaping her.

Suddenly, I wanted very much to cry. It might be safe to do so. My father might think all the tears were from my grief at leaving him; he need not know they were tears of joy and relief that escape was possible.

"Nana!" The name slipped out too loudly.

Annoyance flickered across my father's face. "Yes, she's coming." But I could think of no other way to work it out. I'd heard the arguments, the stepmother's rage that my mother's mother, my Nana, was coming.

I hoped the darkness hid the smile that tried to control the corners of my mouth. I masked it further with a sham yawn, and I was carried to bed.

4

The Birthday Cake

After my mother died when I was two years old, my father sent me to live with various relatives. Because of the treatment I received and the verbal and/or nonverbal messages I perceived, I concluded early on that I never should have been born.

I dreaded my birthdays; no one ever seemed to notice or celebrate them. I saw other children being treated to cake, parties, presents, and other special notice on "their" days. I yearned to receive such affection on my birthdays. The treatment I did receive seemed to say no one was happy to have me around. Except Nana.

The one positive constant influence in my life was Nana, my maternal grandmother. She loved me fiercely and unfailingly. Nana was so insistent that God loved me that I sometimes believed God just might love me too. I imagined God's love to be like Nana's: a steady, positive regard no matter what.

God was very real to Nana. At her home, I felt God's presence. Her Bible, always open on a little footstool by her chair, was a reminder that God was near. In constant pain from rheumatoid arthritis, Nana knew God was her rock, her friend, her strength, her hope. Nana introduced me to her loving God and taught me to pray. On weekends when I was blessed to stay with Nana, God became real to me too. I learned to talk with God and to be at peace because of God's presence.

On the year I turned seven, I discovered that my birthday fell on a Saturday. This meant I would be at Nana's! The Friday morning before my birthday, I got up extra early to pack my scuffed suitcase. The school day seemed endless, but finally, the school bus deposited me at the end of our land. I dashed to the tall frame farmhouse where I spent weekdays with my mother's sister and her family, dragged my suitcase from my bedroom to the kitchen door, then quickly completed my chores.

I came to stand hopefully beside my suitcase. I knew better than to nag or whine but hoped to show my aunt I was ready. Finally, she picked up her purse and car keys, and gave me the look that said she was ready too. I raced for the car and managed to get the suitcase onto the back seat. After what seemed forever, we reached Nana's little home, and I was deposited at the curb with my suitcase.

As always, Nana was watching for me from the large living room window. Her warm hug and gentle words of welcome were like a healing balm. I was at home.

Early the next day, Nana was beside my bed as I awoke. She greeted me with her usual good morning, then added the words I yearned to hear. "Happy birthday! I'm so glad God sent you to me." The warmth of that greeting stayed with me all morning.

Early in the afternoon, Nana told me I was to go to Mrs. Potter, a neighbor at the end of the block, to fetch something. This wasn't unusual, for walking caused Nana great pain in her swollen joints. I often ran errands for her. That day I expected I would be bringing back the usual cup of sugar to replace what the neighbor had borrowed or a bit of inspirational reading or a recipe.

Bundling me up in my heavy coat and mittens, Nana sent me out into the frigid air. My breath rose in clouds of steam as I hurried to Mrs. Potter's little green house and knocked on the door. She invited me in. The fragrance of vanilla and baking filled the room. Mrs. Potter set a box into my outstretched hands. "Be very careful!" she called out as she opened the front door. Then, just as I started to leave, she added, "Happy birthday, Mary. God bless you. Your grandmother is so fortunate to have you help her on the weekends."

The warm glow from Mrs. Potter's words wrapped me all the way back to Nana's door. When she had carefully received the white box, Nana told me to take off my coat and mittens and join her in the kitchen. I did as instructed, then hurried to follow her.

I gasped as I entered the kitchen, for there in the center of Nana's table was a cake. Deep swirls of fluffy, white frosting covered it. Seven candles stood in an arc above the center, and "Happy Birthday Mary" had been written across with pink frosting. I was awed by the beauty of my first birthday cake and the neighbor's kindness. Mrs. Potter, knowing my grandmother's hands were too crippled by arthritis to allow her to do the beating necessary to make the cake and fluffy frosting, had given her time and her own hands to the project.

The cake deeply touched me. It was visible proof that somebody was glad I'd been born. The kindness of Mrs. Potter fed my spirit. The grandmother who knew how deeply I yearned to be loved and treasured nurtured and strengthened my soul.

Because of Nana, I now understand that people may believe God loves them only if a person loves them unconditionally. Nana's fierce and consistent love still gives me hope in the midst of adversity, strength in the face of trouble, and a grateful heart in all situations.

The image of my first birthday cake is still clearly etched in my mind after so many years. It remains a lovely sign of God's love.

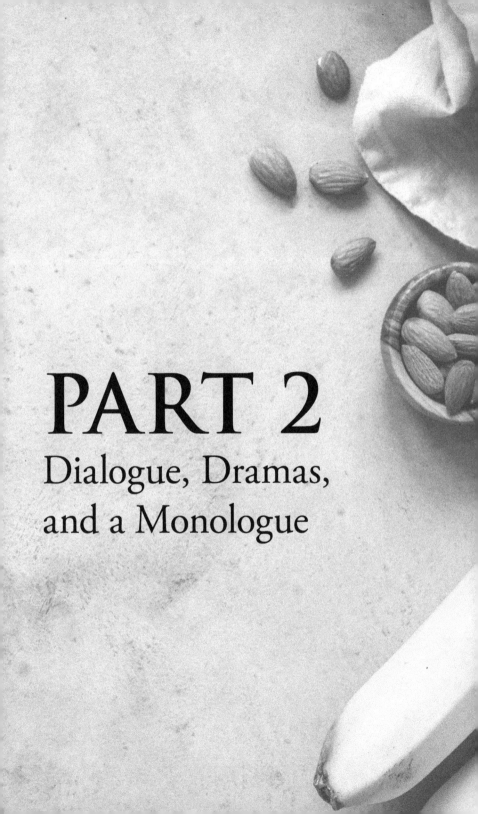

PART 2
Dialogue, Dramas,
and a Monologue

5

Between Sisters

The Persons in the Play
Martha
Mary

Based on Luke 10:38–42 (*Scene opens in a sparsely furnished home with a kitchen center stage. Martha is busy at a small table in a cooking area. She appears to be making bread dough. Her movements are strong; she moves quickly and surely about, obviously at home in her kitchen and with her tasks. This is her domain. Mary enters stage left, with her arms loaded with books. Her face tenses, taking on anxiety or fear, as she notices Martha. Mary tries to slip across the area to another exit without being seen, but the stack of books starts to slip from her grasp and crashes to the floor.*)

MARTHA, (*turning and looking at Mary with disgust.*) So, you've finally come back! Where have you been? Don't you realize I could use some help? Why do you expect me to do all the work here while you act as if you are a guest in the house?

MARY, *sighing.* Hello, Martha. (*Begins again to ease toward the exit, as if still trying to escape the kitchen.*) I … I have some things to do. (*Starts to bolt toward the exit, then stops and turns, takes a deep breath, and straightens her shoulders.*)

MARTHA, (*continuing to fling around and pound the bread dough.*) You always have things to do somewhere else. How about helping with the things that need doing right here?

MARY, (*The look on her face changes from fear to resolve. She lays down a few books, which she hasn't already dropped, hesitantly at first but with her voice growing stronger.*) You're right, Martha; there are important things to be done here, and I need to be a part of doing them.

MARTHA, (*looking up in surprise, but suspicion replaces the look of surprise. She looks at Mary for the first time. Her face begins to soften but then tightens into an angry mask again as she turns back to her work. She dumps the dough out of the bowl and kneads the bread with vigor.*) How would you know what needs to be done around here? You've never taken the time to learn, always acting as if you are better than me. I'm just a house slave to you.

MARY, (*with her face becoming sad. She shakes her head in denial, then reaches toward Martha, as if to pat her on the shoulder, but then draws back as if from a hot stove and stands nearby.*) Martha, this isn't easy for me either. I know I'm not much help to you. But do you realize that you've never given me a chance to learn? You are always so competent. You do things so well and so easily. You are so ... *in charge*, and I know I'd never be able to do things as well or the way you want them done.

MARTHA. If that was a compliment, I accept. But you don't learn anything until you try it. Do you think it's been easy for me to learn how to take care of this home? Mother died when we were so young. I hadn't learned much about doing the most basic tasks, let alone how to run a household before mother died. I had to learn it all on my own. You could learn too, if you cared to.

MARY. Maybe I could, Martha. But I've never felt like you wanted to bother to teach me. You always seem so busy, so closed, as if you didn't even want me around. You look so angry or intense or something that I ... I'm scared of you.

MARTHA, (*being shocked enough to finally stop what she's doing and really look at Mary.*) Scared of me! Scared of me? That is ridiculous. Have I ever laid a hand on you? Have I ever punished you for anything?

MARY, (*in a voice rising in strength and intensity.*) Do you realize that you sound like you're my parent, Martha? I hear that superior, judging tone in your voice. You've never let me feel like we were sisters. You always had to be in charge, controlling everything.

MARTHA, (*using a condescending tone, like an adult lecturing a not-too-bright child.*) Somebody had to take charge and take care of you two younger ones. I've never asked to be in charge; I've never wanted to do it all. But somebody had to. You think it's been easy? You think it's not a burden to know the whole village is watching to see whether Martha is taking good care of her brother and sister and their home? I am trying to honor my father and mother—

MARY, (*interrupting.*) Our father and mother.

MARTHA, (*still irritated but also a bit flustered or embarrassed as well.*) You know what I mean. Quit putting words in my mouth. You, the fast talker, the charmer; you with your way with words. Always able to talk so easily to guests, to everyone. Always with plenty of time to listen to people—except me, of course. Mary, the pretty one, the smart one, the sweet one (*with mounting anger, disgust, and a sneer*), the ... the spiritual one. I've never felt like a sister to you because you always act so ... so ... special! (*Her voice continues to rise, and she seems to be near tears.*) How do you think I feel when I see everybody making over you, paying so much attention to you, while I ... I'm just the drudge, the slave, in the kitchen? I just manage the household, do the cooking and cleaning, marketing and mending, while you—

MARY. I always suspected that you resented me, hated me, and didn't want me around. I always felt that I was a burden to you and that you thought I should feel grateful to you. But I didn't feel grateful, and that made me feel guilty. I just tried to stay out of your sight—for both of our sakes. I've resented you for not giving me what I needed most—love.

MARTHA, (*flaring in anger.*) Love! What do you know about love? Have you ever shown any love for me? I give my life to take care of you and

Lazarus, to keep you fed and clothed. Do you know how hard I've had to work to keep a roof over your heads? And you say I don't show my love for you ...

MARY, (*speaking softly, tentatively, after a thoughtful pause.*) I think I understand what you are saying, Martha—that you were showing your love in the way you thought we needed, but I also understand that what I really needed was for you to treat me as if I had value. I need a sense of value, a sense that somebody cares. I've needed a person to listen to me when I had questions, when I was afraid or confused. I've needed somebody to stop and listen—really listen—so that I could dare to pour out my heart. But you were too busy. I wanted a teacher who could help me understand what life is all about. But you were too busy. I needed a guide to show me how to live a righteous but fulfilled life so that when I come to the end of it, I will feel that I have done something that matters. But you were too ... Oh, Martha! You have loved us in the way that seemed right to you, haven't you?

MARTHA. That's more than I can say for you! You've never showed your love for me. You've never bothered to learn how to prepare a meal, how to find the bargains at the market, how to make or launder our garments. You've never cleaned a dish or a room unless I asked you to. If you loved me, you'd pitch in without being asked.

MARY. But I've never known where or how to begin. I've never learned the things you do so well. And when I came to help, I always thought you were looking so disapprovingly that I knew I'd do something wrong and that you'd yell at me.

MARTHA, (*looking sternly at Mary for a few moments but then with the first glimmer of a smile.*) Isn't this about where we began this conversation?

MARY, (*beginning to smile also.*) I think you are right. Where do we go next so we won't keep going in a circle?

MARTHA, (*speaking sarcastically but smiling again.*) You're the one who's good with words. You tell me.

MARY, (*wonderingly*.) That's the first time you've acknowledged that I have gifts. I've always thought you were looking down your nose at what I could do, like speak well and converse about faith. I've always felt that you saw no worth in what I can do well. You've never asked me for anything before, so I thought you believed I had nothing to give, nothing of any value.

MARTHA. Value! What do you know about what it's like to feel that you are of no value? Do people value what I do? Do they notice that I have been able to manage on very limited resources? Did they notice when Lazarus invited Jesus to dinner, and I, thinking I was preparing for four people, managed to stretch what we had into a dinner for eighteen? While you sat there, listening to Jesus, I was rushing to create a decent meal so this family need not be embarrassed because we failed to show appropriate hospitality to our guests ... as you failed!

MARY. I failed?

MARTHA. You were sitting at Jesus's feet, conversing or listening to whatever, and you didn't even offer them a drink of water or to wash their feet. What kind of hospitality is that?

MARY. Oh, Martha, you are right. I didn't think of that. I just wanted to feast on every word Jesus was saying. I could never understand why you weren't interested in listening to him.

MARTHA. Not interested? I'd have loved to sit and listen as you did. The bits of conversation I could hear were very interesting. They made my spirit soar, my heart light. But I had my duty to do.

MARY. Your duty! Just as I always suspected! I always thought it was your *duty* to care for us; I never believed that you did it out of love.

MARTHA, (*wistfully*.) I find it easier to speak of duty than of love.

(*Both women are quiet for a few moments.*)

MARY. I'm sorry, Martha. I wish we both could have listened to every word Jesus spoke all that day and evening until we were filled.

MARTHA, (*speaking lightly, joking.*) But I had to see that your bellies were filled.

MARY, (*smiling and touching Mary's arm.*) You always took good care of us in that way. But my spirit was hungry. I felt as if my mind was dying for lack of challenges, starving for want of ideas. Jesus fed me as I needed to be fed. He sparked my mind and spirit to life. I felt so special when he spoke about how much God loves us. I felt included, valued, treasured, nurtured in ways I hadn't since ...

MARTHA. Since Mother died?

MARY, (*speaking quietly.*) Yes.

MARTHA. Oh, Mary, I can see how much you have missed being nurtured. But I ... I felt so awkward at that in comparison to other tasks. And I didn't want you to think I was trying to take our mother's place.

MARY. Our mother's place? A sister's love would be welcome.

MARTHA, (*speaking softly.*) Yes. Oh, yes!

MARY. And you never thought you received that from me. (*Again, both are silent.*) When Jesus was visiting us, it almost felt as if Father was with us again. He talked with me of holy things, including me in the conversation—me, a woman! Men never include us. Except for Father and Jesus, I've never carried on a conversation about anything really important—you know, about God and life and spiritual things. Men just exclude us from important things.

MARTHA. You're just like them—just like the men who exclude us!

MARY, (*showing shock.*) In what way?

MARTHA. Didn't you hear what you said? You said, the things men talk about are really important, which means that what I do and talk about—cooking, cleaning, mending, sewing, scrimping out a living— are not important. You are just like the men who think what I and other women do has no value. Let's see them take care of themselves. And let's see you use your words and your learning and your ideas to keep this family alive.

MARY. I never realized that before. I have without thought accepted their judgments of us. And even though I resent being devalued, I didn't understand that I was judging you in the same way that they judge us. Forgive me, Martha.

MARTHA. You know, sister, we've never had a conversation like that before. I haven't had a deep conversation like this since …

MARY. Since Mother died?

MARTHA. Father … he used to talk with me, too. He was a practical man, and he appreciated my practical way of looking at life. "You've got a good, level head on your shoulders," he used to say to me. I felt proud and valuable and special. He encouraged me to learn about the practical stuff of daily life. He prepared me as much as anyone could to take care of us after our parents were gone. I miss his guidance and encouragement so much. Maybe that's why I was so resentful that I had too many responsibilities to come to Jesus's feet and listen. I needed to feel valued too, but …

MARY. (*New understanding dawns on her face. She looks at Martha wonderingly.*) You never let yourself shirk your duty, have you? You've spent your life caring for us. You are now long past the age where it's possible for you to marry. (*Softly*) You've given everything up for us.

MARTHA. You *do* understand.

MARY. I'm beginning to. You've helped me stand in your shoes and see things from your point of view. And God's.

MARTHA. God's? What do you mean?

MARY. I remember some of the stories Jesus told about how God loves us. You've loved us like that, Martha. You've kept on loving us and forgiving us, even when we didn't desire it, didn't appreciate it, and didn't realize that your love was there always. I've been so blind. I never recognized what unselfish love you've given us. You've given your life for us. I am grateful. I think I can be a better sister now. At least I'm going to try.

MARTHA. Me too. I've learned so much about you, Mary. And about myself. I never took the time from my duties to realize what you might have needed, what else I might have given you.

MARY. You did the best you could. You did well. You are a very practical, resourceful person. Heaven knows I need someone like you. (*Says thoughtfully after a pause.*) You know, Martha, if we put all out gifts together, we'd have so much. Together we can be an awesome team. If I accept your strengths as valuable, instead of as different and therefore wrong, you help me. I learn from you. If you can accept that my gifts have value and can work with me, we both will benefit. Maybe we could make a covenant to do that.

MARTHA. Maybe ... Yes, I do want to covenant with you. We can learn from one another if we are willing to see each other's strengths as gifts. If we can stop seeing our differences as wrong, accept one another as we are, and celebrate the way God made each of us, we will each be more balanced. If I can appreciate you as you are, and you can appreciate me, we will each become more fully who God intended us to be. You know, Mary, I've never let anybody come this close to me before. No one else knows me and values me as much as you do.

MARY. Except Jesus. Of course. He went on and on about you the night you fed us all. He talked about how strong and giving and competent you were. He said that's the way God wants us to be, giving our lives for one another unselfishly, without counting the cost. Listening to him, I almost began to be ashamed for not appreciating you all these years.

MARTHA. Why didn't you tell me?

MARY. Remember, that was the night you yelled at me. There was no way I was going to talk with you then. And I guess by the time you cooled off, I'd forgotten to tell you. He saw your value and loved you very much. And I am sure you are just as special in God's eyes as well. You certainly honored our father and mother with your life. You've given your life to care for the orphaned—Lazarus and me. Thank you, Martha. Thanks for your care and your caring. Thanks for being patient. (*Smiles in a teasing way.*) Well, mostly patient—with me.

MARTHA, (*saying crisply to hide that Mary's words have touched her.*) That's about enough of that. (*Moves as if to leave.*) I've got work to do.

MARY, (*saying gently.*) Our covenant, Martha.

MARTHA. Oh yes, our covenant, sister. What …? How …?

MARY. How do we begin? What do we say? Maybe we should let God help us. (*Prays.*) O God, thank you for the gift of my sister, Martha. Thank you for her life and for her generous spirit. Help her to feel the love we have for her. Help us to show her more clearly that we value her gifts. Teach us how to support and encourage and care for one another.

MARTHA, (*prays.*) Creator, I thank you for giving me a sister whose spirit is so close to you. Thank you for helping me to hear, understand, accept, and treasure one another. May we live and work together in ways that please you. Help us, together with Lazarus, to draw closer to one another, for in doing so, we will draw closer to you. God, I promise before you to try to do what I've asked you to help us do.

MARY. This is our covenant, God. Help us to keep it.

MARTHA. Amen. Let it be so.

MARY. Amen. And please, dear God, fill our home with your Spirit so we may dwell together in peace. Amen.

MARTHA. (*Smiles and hugs Mary, gently teasing.*) You always have to have the last word?

MARY. (*Returns the hug, also teasing.*) Words are my thing!

(*Mary and Martha stand quietly for a few moments to signal the end of the dialogue.*)*

---

* Mary wrote this short drama for our first women's retreat.

6

John Wesley and the Methodist Movement

The Persons in the Play

Narrator	Reader
John Wesley Hecklers	
Rescuers 1, 2, and 3	Philip Embry
Susanna Wesley	Three Card Players
Charles Wesley	Barbara Heck

Scene 1 (*A house alone on the stage.*)

NARRATOR. On June 17, 1703, John Wesley was born to Susanna and Samuel Wesley. John was one of nineteen children. His father, Samuel, was a priest in the Church of England and the parish of Epworth.

(*Susanna and John on stage sit on the steps and begin to read.*)

NARRATOR. John's mother was a woman of unusual abilities. She taught her children to read and taught them the scriptures.

(*Susanna walks off, and John goes into the house.*)

NARRATOR. When John was about six years old, there was a fire at the rectory at Epworth. When John saw the flames in the room around him, he moved a chair to the window and called for help.

(*John appears at the window and starts yelling.*)

NARRATOR. Two neighbors worked together and rescued John as the flames raged around him.

(*Rescuers 1 and 2 help John from the window, and Rescuer 3 covers him with a blanket, and all leave.*)

NARRATOR. John left home at age ten and went to Charterhouse School until seventeen. He then entered Oxford University. He was a bright and serious student. While at Oxford, John's younger brother, Charles, founded the Holy Club. The group's purpose was to engage in Bible study, prayer, and sharing for the development of higher religious life. John and three of his friends joined Charles in this endeavor. The group also taught poor children and visited prisons. The club was nicknamed "Methodists."

Scene 2 (*Room with a table and chairs, a cross on the table, and the reader in the room with a Bible.*)

NARRATOR. John Wesley returned from the state of Georgia close to despair. His self-discipline and passion for detail in the spiritual life hadn't led him to peace but to restlessness. He asked, "Have I done enough?" Shortly after his return, Wesley spoke with Moravian Peter Bohler, who told him to get rid of the philosophy and preach until he had faith and, once getting it, preach faith because he had it.

(*John and Charles enter the room and sit down and listen.*)

NARRATOR. On the evening of May 24, 1738, John went reluctantly to a meeting an Aldersgate Street. During the meeting someone read from Luther's preface to the Epistle to the Romans.

READER. To fulfill the law is to do with willingness and love, the works that the law requires. Such willingness is bestowed upon us by the Holy Spirit through the faith in Jesus Christ. So, faith makes righteousness, for it brings the spirit through the merits of Christ. And the spirit makes the heart free and willing as the law requires, and then good works proceed of themselves from faith.

Grace is the good will or favor of God toward us, which moved God to share Christ and the Holy Spirit with us, begets us anew from God, bringing with it the Holy Spirit. O this faith is a living, busy, active, powerful thing!

Such confidence and personal knowledge of divine grace make the processor joyful, bold, and full of warm affection toward God and all created things,

All of which the Holy Spirit works in us through faith. Pray that God works this faith in you.

(*Charles and the Reader leave.*)

NARRATOR. John Wesley reported the meeting on Aldersgate Street in the following well-known journal entry.

JOHN. In the evening I went very unwillingly to a society in Aldersgate Street, where one was reading Luther's preface to the Epistle to the Romans. About a quarter before nine, while he was describing the change which God works in the heart through faith in Christ, I felt my heart strangely warmed. I felt I did trust in Christ, Christ alone for salvation; and an assurance was given to me that he had taken away my sins, even mine, and saved me from the law of sin and death.

I began to pray with all my might for those who had in a more especial manner despitefully used me and persecuted me. I then testified openly to all there what I now first felt in my heart. But it was not long before the enemy suggested, "This cannot be faith; for where is the joy?" Then I was taught that peace and victory over sin are essential in faith in the Captain of our salvation; but that, as to the transports of joy that usually attend the beginning of it, especially in those who have mourned deeply, God sometimes giveth, sometimes withholdeth them, according to the counsels of his own will.

NARRATOR. This faith experience led John Wesley to share the gospel with power and enthusiasm from the coal mines to the streets of London.

Scene 3 (*Methodist Societies Meeting in England: an empty room with table and three chairs.*)

NARRATOR. John Wesley began taking the message of Christ to the common folk, who suffered from the inhuman effects of industrialization. Conditions were brutal in the factories, mines, prisons, and tenements of eighteenth-century England. Wesley organized the United Society. Later, critics referred to the members of the society as "Methodists" and said the members were too orderly and methodical in their religious lives. John Wesley liked the name and adopted it for the society. All his life, Wesley held with the idea that Methodists were organized into societies but remained loyal to the church while developing their religious life. Methodists believed in prayer, study, and action.

(*John enters with Charles and sits at the table.*)

NARRATOR. Soon the United Society had grown beyond the bounds of a single association. Branch societies were formed in various communities. Each society was subdivided onto classes, over which a leader was placed. (*Enter the two group members. John stands up and starts preaching.*)

NARRATOR. Wesley traveled about the countryside continuously and preached to his classes. The societies became successful when Wesley began preaching in open fields.

(*Enter hecklers, who pass by pointing and laughing.*)

NARRATOR. Although Methodism grew in popularity among the urban poor, miners, and farmers, the Church of England was neither accepting nor receptive to John Wesley's preaching.

(*Exit hecklers.*)

NARRATOR. Methodism outgrew the boundaries of England in 1770, when the first Methodist missionaries were sent to America.

Scene 4 (*Sending the Revival to America: Philip Embry and the Three Card Players are playing cards.*)

NARRATOR. Barbara Heck moved with her family to New York in 1760. She was disappointed that there were no Methodist societies in the city.

(*Barbara enters the room and observes the card players.*)

NARRATOR. One day on a visit out of town, Barbara discovered some settlers playing cards. She believed that the game of cards meant more to the settlers than to the work of the Lord. She became angry.

(*Barbara picks up the cards and throws them on the floor.*)

BARBARA. Philip Embry, you must preach to us, or we shall all go to hell together, and God will require our blood at your hands.

PHILIP. I cannot preach for I have neither a house nor a congregation.

(*All rise. The cards are taken away, a cloth is placed on the table, and a cross is placed on the table. Philip takes the Bible and starts to preach while the others listen.*)

NARRATOR. Such an obstacle didn't stop Barbara. She brought in people to form a congregation and led the construction of a meeting house.

(*Everybody comes in and sits around, listening to Philip.*)

NARRATOR. A letter was sent to John Wesley in England, begging for more preachers. Francis Asbury immediately agreed to go. Asbury and another preacher, Thomas Coke, decided to organize America's growing number of Methodist preachers to best cover the nation's population. On Christmas Eve 1784 in Baltimore, they called for all the Methodist preachers to gather at a conference. Out of that meeting, the Methodist Episcopal Church of America was born. Francis Asbury and Thomas Coke became the church's first bishops, organizing the preachers to spread the gospel across the land.*

---

* Mary wrote this play for the 1989–90 confirmation class at Macomb Wesley United Methodist Church. The confirmation class presented the play during a worship service.

7

The Innkeeper

I stepped outside as things began to slow down, the rich going to their beds, the poor curling in corners. The stars were ablaze! Such beauty almost made one believe for a moment that there was hope for this old world.

I stretched and turned to go inside. Then the baby cried! My, that very pregnant woman for whom we'd had no room must have given birth. Poor kid. What a world to be born into. Again, I turned to go inside, but something drew me to the stable to see the child. God knows it's a rough and tumble world to come into. Least I can do is to go welcome him. And maybe, if there's room in the inn tomorrow, maybe I can find a corner for them. From the looks of them, they can't afford a room, but ... It may be the only gift the little tyke and his folks ever receive.

Hope I'm not getting soft. Can't turn a profit if you're soft. Maybe it's just weariness or the starlight or a lonely old man's wishing life was more than work, work, without any joy. Hope, kindness, laughter—commodities almost as hard to come by as enough bread.

The day is lovely, with huge, fluffy snowflakes drifting down—just enough for beauty, not enough to threaten the safety of travelers.

PART 3

Poems

8

A Psalm of Praise

O God, when my trembling hand
reached out to touch the swollen belly
of our daughter, whom we'd feared was barren,
and I felt the flutter of life
kick and dance within the womb,
then, Creator of all life,
my heart began to sing and praise.

I have stood atop the Grand Canyon
and seen the silver flash of river
far below and seen as far
as eye could see—and farther—
the colored canyons snake
across the earth. And been left cold.
Too big!
I can't relate to such immensity.
The very wind sighed there,
like a soul lost—lost and mad

Ah, now I see why you came
as a tiny babe to a humble maid:
There's a miracle my mind
and heart can grasp ...
Yet wonder enough
to spin my head like the planets.

You're a sly one, God,
to make in tiny miracles
so much of wonder
and in miracles so wondrous
a way for little minds and hearts
to know and love you. Amen.

9

Wordsmith

His heavy-muscled mind is flexed
before the fire of vision.
Cold steel he drags
across the anvil's top.
He studied shapes:
the shape that's seen,
the shape that's yet to be.
He sticks; he bends
reality beneath
the hammer of his voice
until, with eye and ear well-tuned,
a poem he shapes;
then turning quickly, thrusts
the glow-hot iron
into the inky waters,
whence a whoosh of steam
rises from creator
to Creator. Amen.

10

Word Play

I delight in play with the toys of my mind.
I shake them out in shining syllables
to sparkle in the sun. I fling
bold buckets to shiver the sleeper wake.
I nuzzle a nozzle into unsuspecting cracks
of dissention and flood, them a sputter.
Oh, I love words:
cascades,
measured drippings,
torrents,
gushes,
trickles,
puddles,
muddles of alphabet soup of a
vocabularia extraordinaria.

Deliver me from umbrellas
and galoshes of conventional thought
and usage concretized
And algaed stagnation of contemplation
And pollution of erudition.
Give me freshets to splash in,
a creek to dash in.
Let me skinny-dip forever.
I'll flick my mermaid tail at should and oughts
and desert thoughts
and make a rainbow when the light explodes
droplets of couplets.

MARY VICK ROTH

11

Poems Come

Poems come
at the least
convenient times,
like today
when I, with
infection in my head
and prescription
in my pocket,
staggered back
from Searle,
getting sleeted on
as I waited for
the reluctant light
to green.
Snow comes at
inconvenient times,
wetting my paper and daring the ink
to stick,
as I, traffic-dodging,
write the poem
that inconveniently
would be born.
Poems come at the
least convenient times,
like your call.

12

I Met a Poet

I met a poet.
Her skin, I think,
was flesh toned (or one of them).
Eyes ... two there were,
fierce bright, yet ordinary.
And ears, yes, I am sure,
a pair of ears,
quite normal size and hue.

I'd not have marked her out
from others of her race and place
had not some vision spun
from out her muse.
Some song she'd eavesdropped
from the angels
exposed her as a unicorn
entrapped within the world.

MARY VICK ROTH

13

Crazed

His thirsty gaze detects
that crazed spark in your eye.
I bask in your divine madness,
seeking sanity in a crazed world.
The music of some silly stream
falls fresh on one wept dry
in life's asylum.
Your light is darkness
for a world gone mad.
I turn as plant to sun
and seek your nourishment.
My schizoid visions
pull me, Janus like.
I search for truth,
am given lies instead.
Yet hear in your
hysteric-pitched notes
what is—
what truly is.
My soul's ears hear it
as the sheep hear his voice.

14

A Candle Snuffed Too Soon

Dedicated to Dr. Rick Iverson, a parishioner at
Wesley United Methodist Church

A candle snuffed too soon from burning,
A mother, empty armed and yearning.

And where is God?

The Lord of all Life sits by a crib, still empty,
And weeps for a mother's tears.
The Lord of Light walks with a doctor, weary
As He has through all his years.

15

The Rock Collector

He wipes his sweaty
hand upon his jeans
and rummages in his
pockets for the stones.

He'll rub together softly in some ancient rite
then lay about
in pretty patterns on the table of his mind

Until bright poems begin
their flint and sandstone,
gneiss and chalk

Clattering into life,
as when memories and visions,
Conflict and desire strike sparks
we glimpse a vision newly made.

16

Eating an Orange

my sharp, little purse
knife for protection cuts
clean around bifurcating;
the bright fruit cuts then
again until the quadrants
wait poetry/nonfiction/play
writing/fiction. I too

in hope pause peel away pored
skin juice pouring down my
wrist, ripping white, soft
strings away, dead things
of habit or of grace I
brought from home. Tear
flesh from flesh weeping.

mind pierces the membranes
segments dry or juicy
squish between my teeth
I rummage through with my
tongue cursing seeds
which full of promise still
set the mind on edge.

17

I Stole a Spoon

I stole a spoon
to stir my dreams
hunched over
hot caffeine
illicitly brewed
on my dorm
room desk.

I stirred in a memory
of cows on green hillside
with the cream
soured now
and the sugar
of a first lover's kiss
turned saccharine.

The spoon handle danced
through a veil of steam-
dimmed memories.
I'll remember dreams,
near dead, stirred
to momentary life
that sent to mingle with the bitter grounds.

18

Spring, Sprung!

Spring, sprung, crowds out promise
with not-quite fulfillment.
Crowded!
Leaf on leaf of greening boughs
obscuring May-bright sky,
dulled dogwood,
fading redbud,
fallen magnolia.

So must we look to God,
our new-minted promise
faded, fallen, wilted,
potential never become.
Does God weep to see
our spring thus sprung?

19

Serve Gently with Vinegar and Oil

A church is like a good salad,
needing *both* vinegar and oil.
The oil of healing,
fragrant with love, reconciles, soothes, heals.
But we need a dash of vinegar
for sharpness,
for confronting us
with reality,
for embarrassing us
out of blind do-goodism
and saccharin piety.

And a toss ...
Now and again we need
a conflict to stir us,
to let truth break in
with reality.
A good salad needs
both vinegar and oil.

20

You Are with Me

Images kaleidoscope across my mind,
scenes of sisters far away in seminary.
I hold the hand of a dying man
and hear in his rough, rasping breath
the throaty whispers of you who comforted me
when life seemed dark as death.
I wait beside the woman, stiff with fear,
whose now-alien body harbors cells gone mad.
And in my silent vigil feel
the touch of your soft hands upon my shoulder.
I weep beside a dying child
and clasp her mother close,
strengthened by the clasp
of your love upon my spirit.
Oh, sisters, in what I am
and who I am
and everywhere I am,
you, too, keep vigil.
Your words and your love,
they comfort me
in the valley of the Shadow of Death.

Images kaleidoscope across my mind,
scenes of sisters not far away
but here.
My cup runneth over;
I do not want for comfort.

MARY VICK ROTH

21

Rainbow Maker

God of palette and brush so wide
flung her brush from side to side,
    made a rainbow in the air,
    sign of God's eternal care.

From the ocean depths below
    found the deepest indigo,
    yellow from the daffodils,
    purple from a thousand hills,
    green from forest glen and grass,
blue from sky where no clouds pass,
    orange and gaudy sunset eves,
red of autumn's brightest leaves—
    These all gave the colors rare
    to paint the rainbow in the air.

God of palette and brush so wide
flung her brush from side to side,
    made a rainbow in the air,
    sign of God's eternal care

22

Fill Us, Holy Spirit

With sighs too deep for words,
like the howling of the winter wind
above the distant threat of wolf cries,
we wail our grief for the world's pain.

We sigh the passion of broken lives,
spewing forth our troubled visions,
exorcising children battered; women
raped, homeless; men seeking to be whole.

Emptied by weeping and sighs too deep
for words, we cry: Fill us, Holy Spirit.
Inspire that we may dare to look again,
to see life's pain and reach a helping hand.

23

Sympathetic Vibrations

Once I fled my children's music
up the stairs and down the hall.
Closing the door, I'd pause to let
the drumming of my heart
return to mannered rhythms.
I'd lean against the wall
and hear it coursing through
the timbers of the walls and floor,
the primal beat.
My heart to the music would leap.

And so it is when I hear
your deep cry that washes in
from dark Stygean shore
and rushes forth from your breaking heart
to issue as a sigh.
My heart in ancient response cries forth.
Every molecule vibrates
in primal response,
like cats and dogs with hair on end;
in sympathetic vibration
I tremble to the intensity of your moan.

My heart cries peace to your heart.
Peace, but do not be still,
for I would share
in sympathetic vibration
your burden, dance the dance
of giving, loving, caring
beside you.

24

The Grass Remembers

The grass remembers
friends of long ago,
who, coming to share cares
and coffee,
a path had trod
across our lawns.

The grass remembers
and memorializes dead friendships
in barren trail ungreened,
a tiny Oregon trail
no spring can erase.

The grass remembers
where once our children played,
once beaten bare
by dancing, running feet
and knees and bodies
abused and awed by life.
The grass hung back
until the restless clover
moved into homestead there.

The grass remembers
my wandering, once-young feet
wandering past the wildflower garden
to the corner point, where dog and I,
could await three school-wearied faces
rushing home to puppy kisses,
chocolate-chip cookies, and mother ears
to fill with such adventures.

The grass remembers
As do I.

25

Going Home

Flat prairie fades away;
excitement flare as first hills appear.
The red earth, spilt and broken, smiles,
while winding roads beckon home.
Insinuations of wood smoke sift
upon the rain-drenched air;
snow-and-ice images melt into memory.
Past pitch of hills, a flicker of curves,
a vista opens of ridge upon ridge
of blues and blues and grays
of hill upon hill beyond hills.
They, hide-and-seeking amidst
cloud-clad air, welcome me home.
I'm going home, past smoky mountains;
the very air, now redolent of pine,
wafts, "Home!"
Familiar mountains, strangled in wintry garb,
evoke the hauntings of my yearning mind:
How are you, my age-ravaged father?
What shall I see in your pain-chasmed face?
The eternal hills, mist shrouded, still,
unblinking, hear my whispers on the wind:

How long? How long do we yet have
to speak of love and treasure one another?
And then the sun comes out;
familiar vistas gleam.
I shake aside thoughts of grim mortality.
The ghosts and fears of early dawn
withdrawn a space till evening.
Home! I'm almost home.

MARY VICK ROTH

26

Shaman's Joke

When you at last permitted me to come,
to hold your hand and wait beside your bed
for death, the great gray wolf, to come, and close your eyes,
I watched how, through the night,
the Shaman came and, with his cosmic laugh,
revealed to all that which, with every breath, you'd taught me to deny.

He danced until the hollows of your eyes,
the great beaked nose, revealed
their Cherokee;
the darkening of your skin revealed
its tribe.
And I, constrained throughout my life
by family and region,
where color was a thing of shame,
I watched your waning heart
beat like the primal drums
of him you had danced.
And when at last your eyelids closed in death,
I fled to walk the forest path,
to watch the great hawk
circling in the sky,
to dance and shout your spirit home.

Now that you lie pride and shame no
longer distress,
I wear the tokens of my kin
and hear in the hawk's sharp cry,
the clattering autumn leaves,
the chuckle of the Shaman
whose joke brings healing
to my grieving heart.

MARY VICK ROTH

27

I Hung Up My Paddle and …

I hung up my paddle …
and I'm drifting … I feel …

All at sea?

Seriously, God, *please.*
I'm trying to sort out my feelings.

Tell me.

Well, I hung up my paddle
after eighteen years. I hung it up.
And I turned my canoeing clothes,
and my summers will never be the same.
I gave up a part of my life.
An era is over.
I'm … grieving.

Yes, that's it: I'm grieving.
I feel loss for … what?
My youth? A tradition?

My wife and I, my children and I …
we all had summers of cannoning.
Am I grieving for the past?
My past? Our past?

The past is past. Time flows on.

Yes, time flows on, and ...

and you don't have a paddle?

Yes, and I ...
Oh!
Oh, yes, God. And I
have no power to ...
Did you ever?
Did you imagine that the small paddle,
that fragile piece of wood,
was directing the course of your life?

I guess that's what I must have imagined.

Did you imagine that the frail craft,
that little canoe,
was transporting you through
the crosscurrents of Life
and that you were propelling
and guiding it?

God, forgive me!
Yes, I sometimes forgot why you ...
So, I only imagined that I ...
Okay.
I hung up my paddle,
left my canoe on the shore,
And ... Now what, God?
You have always directed me,
Direct me now.

There are other vessels.
Climb aboard.

Other vessels?
A dingy. A battleship.
A yacht. An ocean liner.
A ...

You choose, Captain and Pilot
of my life.

The voyage has not ended, you see.

Yes, I understand ... now.

And the "and"?

The "and"? Oh, yes, the "and."
I hung up my paddle, and
the dog died.

Our children had *grown up*,
bright hope in parents' eyes,
but the dog *died.*
The children had left home's safe harbor
and set out, each in his or her own
shiny craft,
each on his or her own individual course.
and we had stood at the door
and waved them on,
rejoicing bon voyage.
But the dog had *died.*
The little companion of our home
grew frail, and heart failed
one day when we were gone.
And we came home to silence,
and death curled like a presence
on the rug before the fire.

And?

And now in the autumn dark,
I cling to my life's companion
and shiver against the howl
of winter's first chill breath
and remember that the dog died.

And?

And ... Yes, I know,
and life goes on.
But life goes on for me
with the echoes of clicking toenails
on linoleum
sounding like time's ticking
in my ears.
And the weary wheeze of aging breath
Remembered reminds me of my own mortality,
reminds me of the rattle
of my dear companion's laboring lungs,
And ...

And?

And life is so good that I cling,
wanting to squeeze the last drop
of joy from each day,
wanting a perpetuation of days ...

And?

And yearn, hope, demand,
An Eternity of Joy.

And?

28

Among the Sheltering Leaves?

Apple, woman, man, what is
that great Big Sin?
Did you think it was only
enjoying one another,
devouring, satisfying appetites?

What of bigger sins than lust?
What of wanting to be God?
What of worshipping not Creator,
but creation?
What of losing God
among the sheltering leaves?

Apple, woman, Man:
Glorify God!
Serves you right to be victims
of mythologizing.

29

Slaughter of the Innocents

They tense in hope,
break forth in joy,
as children finding Christmas things.
Eyes ask one another,
Can it be so?
God's womanhood unwrapped,
Maternal Power acknowledged?
Then we may own our visions,
some inner knowing spoken,
that we, we, too,
created in the Image are.
Can it be so?

So it is, recruiters reassure.
The catalogue affirms:
it can be so!
Hallelujah. God lives!
God's Image Whole
Shines forth!

MARY VICK ROTH

Shines forth …
Shines forth rage,
Distrust.
The thunder of crenelated towers
brought down,
of fortifications breached,
of power usurped,
assumptions kill.

Innocence so newly born
in hope dies young.

30

Cannibal Stew

God, you remember too well my prayers,
especially that prayer of my childhood faith
when fired by missionary zeal.
I begged to take your story
To lost and naked peoples
In some strange and foreign land.

Now here I am, surrounded by cannibals,
Eaten bite-by-bite by others' expectations.
In this black cauldron of demands,
I cringe to see myself devoured,
Too shackled by my shoulds
To flee this mindless martyrdom.

God, deliver me from childish dreams
that I can be all things to everyone.
Teach me humility—that my limits
Are erased only in your limitless Self.
Give me true freedom in the courage to submit;
Give me true strength in the courage to receive.

God, help me to pray only
Thy will be done in me.
Let my mission be the tasks
You choose for me to live in love.
Pluck me out of this cannibal stew
And thrust me into the fire of your service.

31

Weeping for Sarah

From a distance they seemed to be dancing,
circling Sarah's celebrating Spring.
I hastened to join their circle,
yearning for community in their midst.

But as I neared, I learned they weren't dancing.
The circling Sarah showed not joy but fear.
Taut masks bid their faces. Sullen pits
were their eyes, dark with distrust.

Their dance was not a healing dance of joy.
Their movements were mere wrestlings for power,
the pushes, pulls of jealous children fighting,
such as I had only thought to see among men.

Ah Sarah, Sarah,
when will you learn the dance of Life?
When will you claim your strength as healer,
Mender of souls, reconciler, image of God?
When will you cease wresting from your sisters'
remnants of power and claim your own?
Sarah, Sarah, I weep for you.
Sarah, my sister.

32

Quarrel

We quarreled ...
at least I did,
complaining, I'd left;
My home,
the apple trees.
now budding,
The blue sea
of spring flowers,
to follow you ...
into a parsonage,
where I couldn't stretch
both elbows out at once,
couldn't stretch a soul's
length to dance,
where cold walls
echoed back my
Songs in Praise
of you.

　　　MARY VICK ROTH

Then *you* said:
But there's more here
than a dorm room,
and there's a roof
and warmth.
No huddling over grates for warmth,
living out of shopping bags
and standing in line
for a handout meal.

And then I said:
I'm sorry.
Forgive me.

And you said,
"I love you."

33

Digitless

Divine Jesus, digitless,
you wait as I round the stairs.
Where is that pointing
finger of our fathers?
Gone the scolding digit:
"Shame!"
"Sinner!"
Where?

Did some hurting soul
strip away,
circumcise
the judgment rod?

And all remains
an impotent, twisted wire.

Impotent? Not so!
That wire a channel
of Goddess truth.
See how it gestures
Divine blessing,
beckons: Come.

Divine Jesus, digitless,
touch me.

MARY VICK ROTH

34

Somebody's Son Has to Go

Somebody's son has to go ...
To be a visible witness for peace and love,
    To stand before the countless twisted offspring of hatred.

Somebody's son has to say, "No more."
    No more may you oppress.
    No more may you tread upon the bowed necks of the poor.
    No more may you exploit the powerless.

Somebody's son has to stop ...
    The grinding thoughtless system, fueled by greed,
    The monster stirred by suspicion and fed distrust.

Somebody's son has to care ...
    That the dream of a just world does not die,
    That the vision of a new age of peace and unity be lifted up.
    That the hope of swords, become plowshares, shall be remembered.

Somebody's son has to care.
Somebody's son did. And he died.
And now?
My son says he has to go.
And I'm afraid.
And proud.

35

They're Here

A tumble of grandchildren
clutter the floor
with sleeping bags,
story books,
a dolly or four.
The long trip is over,
they're tired to the core.
They litter the carpet
at Nana's once more.
The soft, sighing whisper
of each baby's breath,
more lovely than music,
fills old Nana's breast.
With joy unsurpassed,
with peace that goes deep,
when grandkids come calling,
the whole world can keep.

36

I'd Rather

Fireflies flicker, catch fire,
strew sparks across the sky,
darkened with the pain
of our existence.
These flicks of fire,
struck from stone on stone,
we take for granite
as we bumble
like bugs into summer.
Window screens
and wick and flame
in passionless deaths flare.
I rather be a meteor,
falling, flaming through the air
than circle cold and dark and lifeless
through eternity,
untouched, untouching,
unwarmed, unwarming.
Fireless flick sparks across
the dark, chaotic cosmos
until at last in thunderous
conflagration of response
dawn breaks.
For one brief candle burn
we see.
Then darkness
and only fireflies flickering.

37

Examination

"Deep breaths," he muttered,
thrusting the cold stethoscope
against my ribs.
My shiver rattles the paper gown
that scratches my nape and nipples.

Breathe, breathe.
My vision blurs as mix too rich
fills my lungs.
I strive to focus on the fixed point
as the world begins to spin.
I focus on the point between his eyes
where a frown of—weariness? Concern?—
Disturbs.
Examination done, I close my eyes.
I do not want to know what knots his brow.
Examination done, he mumbles, "You can
get dressed now." His voice, colder than the
stethoscope, sets me shivering again.

38

Beside the River

We watched the rhythmic ripples,
observed the water birds
walk to and fro, pursuing fish,
the gulls cry overhead.
So like the conjunction of our lives,
the peace of clouds above us drifting
brought mingled sun and shade
upon our heads.

So like the joy and grief
flowing over our lives,
mingled forever together.
We laughed and loved.
We wept and wondered.
Caught in some perfect moment blessed,
indelibly stamped on glowing tones
beside the river of memory.

39

Thou Beauteous Instrument

I've heard the sounds at Autumn sing
    death's prelude through a thousand trees.
I've heard a symphony of robins weave
    their song of hope in winter-wearied air.
I've mourned the drum of dying dreams all dashed
    to dust among the ashes of lost youth.
I've crooned the dying prayerfully on their way
    and heard life's last breath hiss to silence.
I've borne the cacophonic chorus of the lost,
    the lone, helpless, and oppressed,
      who've raged and wept and railed and wondered.
I've been swept by angelic choirs and heavenly strains
    of violins to heights so rare and wonder filled
    I thought I'd glimpsed the face of God.

Yet none of these has so intensely touched or moved
    or higher borne, nor plunged to darker depths,
      nor swept in wilder currents mingling grief and joy,
    my deepest unplumbed self,
than your sigh, too deep for words,
    that gathers all the pain and grief
    and torment of a brutish world.
And in a rush sweeps clean the threshold of my mind
    and fans the faint, guttering spark
of all I seek and yearn and dream might be.

What is this sigh that seems to drag
    with power more telling than the tides?
It seems for wind to draw the very breath of God.
For instrument, your soul,
    crafted and carved by a caring Creator,
    sounds forth with love so rich
    that corridors and courts
    are sounding boards and frets.
And firmaments and fathomless depths of sea and spaces and time
    resound, awake and tremble, resonate, rejoice.

Ah, thou beauteous instrument, play on.
Let your deep-healing sighs sweep, surround,
    smite, soothe, shake, succor me
till, tempest tossed, I slip into momentary lull.
And with the falling of my tears I shall be whole.
Then, thou healing friend, my peace flows in to fill
    the empty, aching places of your self
    from whence the sigh rolled forth.
And you and I float tranquil, star canopied, and blessed,
borne on a raft of friendship deep as any sigh,
the universe our lake, over which, like the lost loon's call,
deep bass notes of caring, contrapuntal melody of laughter,
with strong harmonious notes of trust, shall shiver into song—
with some divine duet as yet unheard, we'll greet the dawn.

40

If

If you were a kite
    and I the tail,
We'd soar away together.
The wind would lift us,
    as our love does now
when we are together.

If you were the kite
    and I the tail,
we'd spar together.
The sun would warm us
    as our love does now.
The ground would shrink,
    as my fears do now,
when we are together.

41

I Might

I might have had a dwelling without you,
but such a wretched hovel and so cold
    would any mansion be without your love
    to warm the empty space, to make it home
    with your dear, fierce embrace
    of greeting at the door.

I might have had a garden without you
    with meandering rows and barren space,
    where with your love alone you'd make it grow.
    And flavorless the food, colorless the flowers,
except you brought them dewy-offered into me.

I might have had a song to sing without you
    but such a monotonal melody sans meaning
    and flat without your lilt and rhythm.
    Without your riching harmonies, I'd have
    no cause for singing lustily through life.

I might have found a way to go without you
    but wander purposeless throughout eternity,
    without a way of going, without light
    or laughter on my way alone,
    I'd have dwelt in darkness all my days.

I might have known my God without you.
    But distant, cold, and stone my god would be.
    Except God may be manifest in you, except you mirror God's self-
    giving love,
    how should I find belief in God?

I might have had a life full to the brim,
    as some would measure fullness in a life.

I might have riches, travel, and friends untold,
    but such a life would poor and empty be
    unless enriched with your dear self.
I might have had all things. Without you,
all things would nothing be.

42

How Long I Waited

How long I waited,
setting the unclaimed place at my table.
Watching. Peering surreptitiously
beneath the half-drawn curtain of my lashes.
Watching that I might see the first
slightest turning toward me,
the smallest acknowledgement
that you knew I still exist,
that you were coming
to dine on conversation,
to laugh and comfort. To hear.
Grasping the laden bunches
of words from my lips
that would spill from
a heart too full of living,
weeping and laughing
and sighing to contain.

How long I waited before vain hope ceased to blind my eyes,
and I could see your life was full.
You banqueted on others' words
and murmured consolations in others' ears.
I gather up the crumbs,
set right the solitary table and …
How long? I waited.

43

A Starry Night and You

The moon is a fingernail clipping
upon the navy carpet of the night,
where dark angels drag their feet
and strike sparks.

And you beside me
sigh from some deep
darker and more mysterious than the moon.
Your eyes alight;
you turn to me and strike sparks.

MARY VICK ROTH

44

The Rose

It began as a bud,
the potential not apparent
in the small, green bit,
hard and unpromising.

The first bright glimpse
of hope pinked
when you awoke, approached,
and bared your soul to me.

A petal stretched
toward the light
of your brave spirit
reaching out to me.

The blooming came
as I responded,
and love flamed and fired
when spirit, spirit struck.
Now crimson flames
into full bloom.
All fragrance and beauty
enfold us together.

The rose glows with joy
beyond expectation,
fierce passion unpredicted.
We grasp and scarcely feel the thorn.

45

The Necklace

As two lives brushed in passing,
we paused and glanced and caught
in gaze to gaze some hint
of more than passing by.
A necklace we began
of moment to moments strung
upon a rawhide thong:
Each time based slid and clicked,
a gentle cricket's call,
together.

See how each bead is scored
with memory we shared:
This one imprinted faint
by some primeval fern
to chronicle when once we hung
above a wooded gorge
to raven-view the world.
Here's one etched sharp and bold
in strange geometry,
memento of some discord eased
by sharing each to each.

And here's a sea star brand
evoking sea songs once I sang
to rescue you from some
deserted isle of mind.

MARY VICK ROTH

With tracery of lace,
this satin orb is scored
to mark the ordinary days
made finer with a smile.
See here's a tendril curling,
and here a leaf and vine,
mementos of a chilly eve
made warm with talk and wine.
This amber glow suspends
three music notes, a score
from some tumultuous tune,
Last vintage scribed in stone
of songs our dancing drummed.
Each bead is different yet
is of a kind in shade,
all friendship colored.

What now shall we who part—
you to your woods and me
a desert path to seek—
do with this memorized strand?
Shall we tight clutch end knots
and let this past pull back
as we yearn future ward?
Or shall we clutch, crone fingered,
the past's crumbs staled and tell
its rosary, "I remember;
I remember," in whispers sibilant?
Or albatross it tangles us
in tired retellings of good
old days until we drown?
Or shall we jerk this thong
to violence it in two
and watch the beads caught still
stop-actioned in our minds
forevermore?

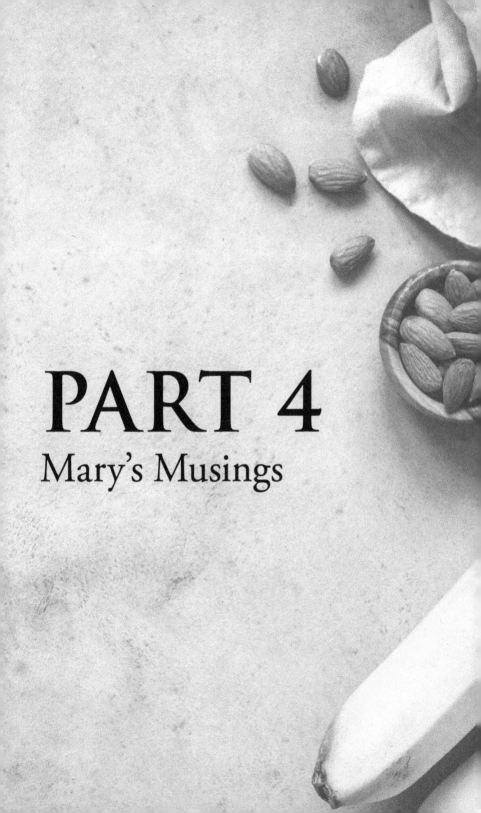

PART 4
Mary's Musings

46

I'm Hooked on the Smell
of New Crayons

I became addicted when I was six, and my grandmother gave me my first-ever-mine-alone brand-new package of forty-eight new crayons. They were beautiful, from their mellow, waxy scent to their perfect un-blunted tips and colorful, un-smudged labels. I loved them. I was hooked. To this day, when August rolls around, I can't resist opening a new box of crayons and furtively sneaking a sniff. My reaction is predictable. I hallucinate. I begin to have visions of the kind of year I hope to have or what I hope to accomplish. I have a heightened sense of anticipation and purpose.

As a child, I always hoped for kind and fair teachers. I always vowed to work hard and make good grades. I anticipated that I would learn much of value. Today my visions are no longer about school but about our ministry together here at Wesley United Methodist Church. But the familiar sense of anticipation and excitement about a new year are just as vivid.

There's something of the perpetual child in me, I guess. Call it faith; call it hope. No matter how many school years ended, I trudged home with a battered box full of broken crayons, most missing their papers, so I couldn't tell what color they were any longer. But no matter how many dreams and hopes had gone unrealized that year, still when August came—when August comes—there's still a new box of crayons, a new year, new possibilities for new beginnings, and fulfilled dreams.

47

The Old Redbud Tree and Us

The tree had grown tall for a redbud. Its trunk was spindly. Weak branches drooped onto the parsonage roof, where every wind caused them to scrape against the shingles. The tree, which had grown without pruning, was weak and vulnerable, damaging what it encountered.

How much like us, it is, I thought as I watched it being cut down. When we grow without pruning away unhealthy attitudes and self-interests, we, too, grow up weak and unstable, hurting ourselves and others. The redbud would have been a healthy tree, strong and vigorous, if it had been pruned, trained, and formed into a disciplined plant.

And we, too, become strong and spiritually healthy, giving glory to God only when we submit to the instruction of the Bible and discipline ourselves to live after the example and teachings of Jesus Christ.

I felt sad as I watched the redbud topple and fall, knowing we would miss the lovely blossoms in the spring and its shade on warm summer days. *What a waste*, I thought. But I feel a much greater sadness when I see a life wasted through lack of pruning, when neither instruction nor guidance has shaped it, when neither self-discipline nor faith gives it form and value, when neither wisdom nor will keeps it from doing harm to itself and others.

You may think it doesn't matter much that a tree died. Perhaps. But you must agree that it matters when a human life is wasted. That's why we struggle to "prune" our children, isn't it? That's why we presume to speak lovingly to a friend about his or her undisciplined habits. That's why we examine our own lifestyles and prune away what is unhealthy in them. We know that a life wasted is a tragedy.

48

Leaves and Lives

Remember the week when the rain just wouldn't stop? That was the week when the leaves, beat from their precarious twig perches, started to carpet lawns and drives. Golden maple leaves fell from the tree beside the parsonage and stuck in sodden lumps to the concrete walk. When the rain stopped, the leaves dried and blew away. But their "shadows" remained. The heavy rains had leached pigments from the leaves, and where each leaf had lain, its outline was imprinted on the cement. Weeks later the images remain, much as when we touch a life and leave our imprint on it. Whose life did *you* touch today? Whose lives will you touch tomorrow? What kind of images do you leave on others?

Even the beautiful, golden maple leaves left only dull, shadowy etchings on the concrete. But you … you can leave images of life and color and joy, the joy you know in Christ. You can share images of hope and love. What images do you choose to leave?

49

Reflections on God's Grace

Sarah has her first tooth. My father lies dying in the hospital. "...the LORD gave, and the LORD hath taken away; blessed be the name of the LORD" (Job 1:21 KJV). "I know that my redeemer lives" (Job 19:25 NIV). Familiar words. Comforting words. Words that—with your prayers—supported me through Sunday.

Rustled out of bed at four thirty by hospital staff telling me my father had taken a turn for the worse, I stayed with him until it was time to ready the sanctuary and myself for first service. A kind parishioner led my church school class so I could return to the hospital until time to prepare head and heart for second service. Then after worship I was back to sit with Father until time to prepare for the Wesley Forum. Then your prayers and those comforting words really had to supply my strength. What am I saying? I'm saying that God's grace is sufficient. God will bear us up. I'm saying thank you for sharing my burdens. I am saying that "I know whom I have believed, and am persuaded that he is able to keep that which I have committed unto him against that day" (2 Timothy 1:12 KJV). I am saying that I know that my redeemer lives! And that makes all the difference.

Sarah has her first tooth. My father lies dying. And, caught in the middle generation, I listen for the comforting words, sing the songs of faith at his bedside. God smiles with me at Sarah's tooth, weeps with me at the hospital. God supplies all our needs. God still supplies all your needs. Thanks be to God. Amen.*

---

* Sarah is the oldest granddaughter of Mary and Merlin Roth.

50

O Thou Most Kind

The wonder that I am not alone through the watches of the night and the demands of the day causes my tears to fall afresh, O Most Kind.

In the hospital room, where my father struggles to be free of living, I am not alone. In the rattling of his breath, I hear you whisper, Ever-Constant One.

In the soft rustle and clatter of nurses' ministrations, I hear you.

When the moments are endlessly strung one on another until the necklace of the days is wrapped around my throat and I am choking, shivering, and bent with their cruel weight on my shoulders, then you send the One who speaks words of comfort and concern.

O Thou Most Kind, a soft tap on the door frame announces the presence of a friend to ask what he can do to help. Another bears the flowers from the sanctuary, all bronze and gold in a glass jar. Having graced the altar as I preached, they now speak your gracious presence. Their beauty, held in the ordinary vessel, reminds me of your incarnation in the ordinary folks who came to me bearing your love. The doctor's kind and forthright glance as he speaks of what may be … and of you: a gift from Thee, O Thou Most Kind.

The tender, compassionate embrace of a beloved restores my sense of connectedness and relieves the ache of abandonment: a gift from Thee, O Thou Most Kind. In all things, in everything, in life, and in death I find you, present, abiding, and loving God. Because of your love, I am not alone, O Thou Most Kind. Thanks be to you.

51

Love beside the Door

I've always heard that it's afterward—after the formal, scheduled events, such as visitation and funeral, after family and friends go home—that grieving becomes tough. It is so. At least, it's been so for me. Now that I've had time to feel the weariness and pain, I feel it.

True, our faith still sustains, still comforts. But major portions of strength come now from the love I find by the door. I go to the sanctuary alone to play the piano and pray until the healing release of tension begins. I return to find by the door a bag of turnips and apples from a friend who knows of my secret love of turnips. I return from the office to find love by the door: a mailbox jammed with sympathy cards and notes. I enter the office and find love in the form a loaf of bread or a cake by the door. The memo board by the kitchen door is covered with love—the names of those who brought food when we were too weary to prepare meals, who called to invite me to lunch when I needed a break, who called to say, "I'm sorry. I'm praying for you." You have ministered to me and my family in our grief.

Let us together keep learning how to give the love of Christ to one another. And *thank you* for the love beside the door—the love of God made visible by your hands.[*]

---

[*] "Love beside the Door" was written after the death of Mary's father.

52

The Returned Thank-You Note

Among the junk mail lay an envelope with my return address and the cold yellow sticker of the postal service. "Not deliverable. Address unknown." In the envelope was a letter of thanks I had written to my high school Latin teacher. I had written him because he taught me more than Latin. I wrote because at an age when I had struggled between doubt and faith, looking to the adults in my church for proof that it was possible to live faithfully, I found Mr. Long, the image of hope.

But I wrote too late. My thanks were undelivered, undeliverable. Friends told me he had died quietly in his sleep the previous spring.

He never read my testimony of what he had meant to me. His forwarding address was unknown to the U.S. Postal Service. But I know he lives on in my memory and I'm sure in the memory of many others he taught so much.

The last thing I learned from this is, don't wait too long to say thank you. So, on November 23, when we are invited to bring our thanksgiving letters, I'll be ready. I hope you, too, will be ready to say thanks while the letters can still be delivered. Thanks, Mr. Long, I learned.

53

Here I Stand—I Can Do No Less

So said Martin Luther when he realized he could no longer with integrity ignore the corruption of his day. So, I pray, will we all come to say at many points in our faith journey. Where do I stand? This is a question we must keep asking and answering as our faith confronts the issues of each day. And if you ask with honesty, turning the issue this way and that to really examine it with open inquiry, you find that a decision about where you should stand may not come easily. You may take your stand only after much searching, struggle, and pain. Thus, we grow in faith.

Where do I stand? This is a question I keep asking myself and answering as my faith confronts the issues of each day. And decisions come only after much prayer and pain. Thus, I grow in faith. Here I stand. I don't tell you what to think, but I challenge you to think with integrity, prayer, soul-searching, and scripture searching. I don't ask you to follow me. I challenge you to follow Christ. And together may we pray with our lives, "Thy kingdom come in earth as it is in heaven" (Matthew 6:10 KJV).

54

Straightening the Candles

Alice Davis recently polished the brass candelabra. I met her in the dim, cool sanctuary on Saturday morning to reassemble and stand them on the altar. We put new beeswax candles in, seven for each candlestick, stepping back often to be certain each was placed perfectly upright. At last, when Alice and I stood behind the altar and sighted toward the narthex, we saw fourteen tall parallel candles in softly gleaming brass holders. "There," she said.

"Wait," I answered, motioning her to stand at the end of the altar.

"Ah, I see." She smiled. "When you sit over there," she added, pointing to the liturgists' chairs, you can see that the candles are not really straight."

"That doesn't matter," I responded. "What matters is that God can see." We continued to adjust the candles, looking at them from all directions, until they were straight.

As I walked home afterward, I thought we are just like those candles: from one point of view—our own—we may appear upright, while from where others—family, coworkers, friends—stand, we may not appear upright at all.

What shall we do then? Make a fearfully honest inventory. Quit kidding ourselves. Pray that God will change us. Strive to be honest and upright in all our relationships—including with ourselves. And give thanks to the God who loves us, even while we are sinners.

"Straightening the candles" is a lifetime job, but we don't work alone. God works with us. And God's great transforming grace is greater than all our sin. Thanks be to God.

55

From Lent to Advent

The last thank-you note is written, and I put the memorial book for my father away. I begin to reread the sympathy cards and letters. They fill a large basket, so I throw away the envelopes of cards from folks whose addresses I know. I tuck the cards into the large, white envelope with the funeral book, taking out a few that seem to require a letter in response. Then I sort through a few more papers concerning estate business filing most and setting aside a few for attention. The file, the large white envelope, is put away.

The table where I've worked for one and one-half months looks empty except for a fading pink azalea, the last of the flowers. I am empty. The few papers I've placed on my desk mean the work will go on. I will go on; life goes on.

But I am in Lent, and the world is in Advent. I go to the florist and find a wreath for the front door. Its circle signifies God's endless love. I play Handel's *Messiah* on the stereo and let the rich message of hope and joy roll over me. I take two needy children shopping and begin to feel rich indeed. Then I sit by the fireplace, where my carefully laid fire begins to emit a cherry warm. Darkness begins to fall. A vague disquiet makes me squirm. The candles! Why are there no Advent candles in the windows as a sign of welcome? What if Christ came and found my lamp unlit? But I am not ready. I am in …

Ah! I dash up the stairs and rummage through the Christmas boxes in the guest room closet, through box after box of ornaments, decorations, saved through the years. At last, I find the ones I want. Leaving most of the collection behind, I hurry downstairs. Soon candles gleam from the windows, the lighted ceramic church glows from the mantel, and the small, simple crèche shines in the light of a single candle on the table.

It is enough. My home speaks of what is most important to me: hospitality, hope, and joy. I am in Advent.

56

Our Lenten Journey

If every journey begins with a single step, we have begun our Lenten journey. The ashes of Ash Wednesday have been washed away. Many of us have begun reading the Bible lessons for Lent in our purple Lenten booklets. Some of us have given up something for Lent. Others of us have taken on something for Lent—some task, some good deed, some act to bless another in Jesus's name.

Scripture tells us that Jesus "set his face to go to Jerusalem" (Luke 9:53 NRSV). That means, of course, that even though he knew what lay ahead, he was determined to suffer and die to fulfill the mission before him. He didn't turn away; he didn't hesitate, even though he knew the road ahead was a lonely and challenging one.

Have you set your face toward Jerusalem? Have you made a commitment to go where God wants you to go and do what God wants you to do, even though you will be challenged and face hardships?

What is your Jerusalem? Is it at home, where you are constantly challenged by an uncooperative spouse or disobedient children? Is it at work, where your efforts are unappreciated and your coworkers are difficult? Is it within you, a place where you need to "go" to see what lies within you? Do you need to face some shame or guilt for which you need to forgive yourself? Do you need to face a habit or practice that isn't in line with your Christian convictions?

How is it with your soul this Lent? Do you need to invite God or a Christian friend to walk with you and hold you accountable? Remember, even on our Lenten journey, we never walk alone.

57

A Long Song for Disciples

Twenty years ago, Eugene H. Peterson wrote a fascinating book *A Long Obedience in the Same Direction Discipleship in an Instant Society*. The book focuses on the fifteen "Songs of Ascents" (Psalms 120–134). These fifteen psalms were likely sung, possibly in sequence by Hebrew pilgrims as they went up to Jerusalem to the great worship festivals. Three times a year, faithful Hebrews made the trip (Exodus 23:14–17; 34:22–24). The Hebrews were a people whose salvation was accomplished in the exodus, whose identity was defined at Sinai, and whose preservation was assured in the forty years of wilderness wandering. When these people regularly climbed the road to Jerusalem to worship, they refreshed their memories of God's saving ways at the Feast of Passover in the spring, they renewed their commitments as God's covenanted people as the Feast of Pentecost in early summer, and they responded as a blessed community to the best God had for them in the Feast of Tabernacles in the autumn.[2]

The picture of the Hebrews singing these fifteen psalms as they left their daily routines and made their way from towns and villages, farms, and cities as pilgrims up to Jerusalem has become embedded in the Christian devotional imagination. It is our best background for understanding life as a faith journey. If we learn to sing them well, these psalms can be light and lift us in our walk as disciples. There are no better "songs for the road" for those who travel the way in faith with Christ, a way that has so many continuities with the way of Israel. Since many essential items in Christian discipleship are incorporated in these songs, they provide a way to remember who we are and where we are going.

We are familiar with that long obedience of climbing long distances to worship God. Thus, we may not feel the need to mine them for wisdom and sing them for cheerfulness as God's people did long ago. We want instant

MARY VICK ROTH

satisfaction, instant grace. We are not interested in the long obedience of lifelong growing as disciples of Christ. But when God grows an oak, he takes a hundred years. When God grows a squash, he takes only a couple of months. The question is, which would we rather be—oaks or squashes?

God knows we have much to learn about encouraging and teaching one another for the long obedience. As we move from comfort zones into new realities, to which God is leading us, we need new songs to lift our hearts and spirits. We need to prepare for a marathon of faithfulness. We might think of Lent as a forty-day practice to strengthen us for long-term faithful living throughout our lives. Choose your song, and let's move out on faith. Emery Austin said, "Some days there won't be a song in your heart. Sing anyway!"

58

A Lenten Message for You

I was a child enjoying a warm day in late April. I lay on the new grass, peering at ant level through the green sprigs, past hundreds of smiling dandelions. Their fragrance mingled with the scent of apple blossoms and the smell of damp earth. I turned and turned, seeing yellow flowers and grass stretching in every direction. "I'm the center of the universe," I murmured to myself as I rolled over and saw the sky stretching over me in every direction. "I think I'm the center of the universe," I said aloud, then laughed to ease a sudden terror. I had glimpsed the awful truth: I wasn't the center of the universe.   And then it was over. No more could I pretend that everything in creation revolved around me. Everybody else thought he or she was the center and had as much—or as little—claim as I. I'd caught myself in idolatry; I was exposed. Life would never be the same again. I would never be the same—or the center!

I can wish nothing more precious or profound for you this Lenten season than that you discover yourself in your own idolatries. And that, having discovered them, you can never again believe in them. May you this Lent have some quiet discovery or some soul-jolting surprise awareness that humbles you, stirs you away from your idols, and throw you wholly, humbly on the merciful, loving, and forgiving Center of all, our Lord and our God.

On the cross, Jesus Christ broke open and exposed every human prideful illusion. The earth shook; time broke apart. Humanity was exposed for all time as self-deceiving and idolatrous. When the clear light of perfect love was shown into the shadowy places of the human heart and illumined the true Center of all things, we were set free to know truth.

59

Cleaning Out the Gutters

The winds and temperamental temperatures of March and early April finally abated enough to give me a warm, sunny day to clean out the gutters. The warm sun warmed my back as I set the ladder against the garage. As I climbed the rungs, I remembered having made this trip the previous autumn, shouting at the trees to let down their last leaves. I wanted to clean out all the leaves and not have leftovers accumulating to freeze in the guttering over winter. But I knew before I peered over the top of the gutter that I'd find them full of those leaves that lurked somewhere in the late autumn until I'd put my ladder away and gone inside. Then, borne by a capricious, laughing wind, they filled gutters and downspouts.

Sure enough. Here was plenty of the residue of winter to scrape away. Leaves and twigs, composited by the action of rain and snow, freezing and thawing into unrecognizable debris, had accumulated. I wondered what unseen pollutants they harbored as I dredged them out into garbage bags.

Cleaning out the gutters is a slimy task. I do it because it needs to be done. The sense of accomplishment I feel comes from knowing how much clogging and pollution—seen and unseen—I can remove in a brief time. It occurs to me that cleaning out our mental gutters of pollutants—seen and unseen—is equally important. The unseen residue was clogging the gutters of my garage. What attitudes do I need to climb up to and clean out?

60

Claiming a More Joyful Life

"Finally, beloved, whatever is true, whatever is honorable, whatever is just, whatever is pure, whatever is pleasing, whatever is commendable, if there be any excellence and if there is anything worthy of praise think about these things" (Philippians 4:8 NRSV).

When you think, think again. When you think there is nothing more you can do to make life richer and more joyful for you and others, think again. When you think, *That's just the way I am*, think again. Know that our Lord and Savior, who invited us into the abundant life through the gift of the Spirit, transforms us and gives us all we need to make the changes we know we need and want. First, avoid criticism and find something to praise in everyone you meet. Thank God for that person. Pray for him or her. And pray for yourself when you forget to avoid criticism. Forgive yourself and keep trying.

Second, look into your own heart before you criticize someone else. Confess to God your own shortcomings before you condemn someone else. Ask God to help you see the good in the one you are judging. Yes, there really is good in the person you most dislike and disrespect. Try to see the person as God does, as his beloved child. There is good in everyone. God made all of us, and God doesn't make junk.

Third, when somebody says to you, "Isn't it terrible what [somebody] did or failed to do or whatever?" respond in these two ways. First, suggest to the critic that he or she talk with the person of whose actions he or she disapproves. Second, find something to praise in the person being criticized. Say to the critic, "Yes, but did you see what a great job she did with [whatever it was]?" Or name some positive quality you see in the person. "Isn't it amazing how, as busy as he is helping people, he never seems to be cross or impatient?"

May God bless you on your spiritual journey. You are following in the footsteps of Jesus. You are not alone, for the Spirit is with you. You need not want for encouragement because members of your church family are ready to pray for you, walk with you, encourage you, and extend a hand. How blessed we are to be Christians!

61

The Toe Lady and Bob

"Now there are varieties of gifts, but the same Spirit, and there are varieties of services, but the same Lord: and there are varieties of activities, but the same God who activates all of them in everyone. To each is given the manifestations of the Spirit for the common good" (1 Corinthians 12:3–7 NRSV).

"Let me see," my daughter demanded.

"No," I answered. "Not here!" Our daughter, Marti, was talking about my toe—my left big toe, which I had discovered that morning to be infected. That toe had been signaling its unhappiness to me for about two weeks, ever since I trimmed my toenails in haste. I'd felt pain grow more and more sharp each passing day, and I'd kept telling myself that I probably needed to examine and trim the nail more carefully. But I didn't take the time, just kept rushing around without checking the source of pain. Then that morning I had finally investigated. My toe was deep red and swollen. An ulcerated area stretched from the point where I'd left a jagged edge of nail to pierce my flesh down to the underside of my toe. No wonder it hurt.

"I know I should have taken better care of myself, but it's so hard to trim that thickened nail," I explained.

"You need the Toe Lady," Marti murmured.

"Who's that?" I asked, watching her face closely to see whether she was joking. "Is that like the Tooth Fairy, only for adults?"

Marti explained that a woman in Bloomington-Normal who went around to nursing homes to cut the toenails of residents was known as the Toe Lady.

I was too intrigued by the thought of this angel of mercy to be offended that my daughter thought I was ready for a nursing home. I imagined the joy I would feel if some caring person were to come to my home and tackle that stubborn, thick toenail so I didn't have to struggle every week or so to clip the rascal into sufficient submission to reduce the pain and avoid infection. I remember my father's apprehension of a friend named Bob who came every week or so and asked in his soft Carolina drawl, "Stuart, would you like me to trim your toenails?" My legally blind father was blessed indeed to have someone who could see and reach and would volunteer.

I've been thinking about Bob and the Toenail Lady and wondering how they found their unique ministries. They must have listened long and carefully to God until they saw the special need, which they could meet. They made a difference in others' lives because they touched others at their point of need. Bob and the Toenail Lady were truly servants of Christ, humbling themselves to do the ordinary, unglamorous, laborious, distasteful (Oh, come on now. You know you wrinkled your nose when you learned I was writing about toenails!) tasks that bring healing and help in a very basic way.

What would the world be like if every Christian first asked, "What do others need that I can give? How can I serve my Lord? How can I help to make another's life a little easier or more pleasant?"

What would the church be like if we dared to offer our humblest talents to meet real human needs rather than to fear that those gifts aren't fine enough? What would happen if we could admit our needs and accept the ministering of one another to the glory of the Giver of all gifts?

I don't think everyone is called to be a trimmer of toenails, a Toe Lady and Bob, but I am convinced that we are all called to be servants. I am certain that God expects us to search creatively, imaginatively, and sensitively to discover however we may use our talents to remedy needs, to bring hope and healing, and gentleness and love for the common good.

As this new year dawns, may you discover to what special use Christ calls your talents to be used, and may you serve with joy. And may God help me find the Toe Lady.

62

Surprise, No Surprise, Surprise

One spring when we lived in Macomb, a friend said, "Come enjoy the beauty of creation on your day off."

"Where are we going?" I asked.

"It's a surprise," she said.

Soon we were zipping south on the River Road from Nauvoo. Redbud and dogwood blooms brightened the roadside. Snowdrops and spring beauties greeted us from the woods. Then we reached Quincy.

I was surprised by gracious homes, carefully preserved architecture, wisely planned expansion, well- maintained public areas, plentiful parks, fine schools—beauty everywhere. I saw Quincy as a town where a proud past is remembered and revered, where life is rich and full in the present, and where the future is anticipated with hope and responsible preparation.

I didn't dream that one day Quincy would be home for us. When superintendent Cinthia Jones told us I was appointed to Quincy Union United Methodist Church, I celebrated a new surprise. I already knew of Union's good qualities from former and present members. So my first response was, "Wonderful!" My second response was a regretful. "But we'll miss spring there!" That regret was instantly erased when I learned the effective date of my appointment was May 1.

We scrambled to locate and purchase a home, packed, and moved all the heavy things (books) and connected with Tom Logsdon (that dear teddy bear with his lively sense of humor and lively confirmands) and Marjorie and Marian. I learned what I needed to know about my ministries so I could hit the ground running soon, soon, soon.

What a lively, energetic, growing, stretching congregation you are! The vitality of your ministry shines in the community. Your leadership, supported by Tom, Gary, Marjorie, and Marian hasn't faltered. Your vision for your future is clear as you focus on the goals you've set for yourselves. The beauty of Quincy in the spring is exciting. The all-season beauty of the Union congregation inspires me: the beauty of your blossoming faith, your service to Christ, and your making new disciples for Christ by the way you live your lives in the community. To me this is the every-season beauty of Union. And we're so eager to join you.

Pray for Merlin and me during the transition. Help us to learn names and faces by wearing your name tag. Share your hopes and dreams for Union. Welcome Merlin by inviting him to play golf. If you don't play golf, ask him his score on the last round in Quincy (if you have time to hear his response). Express appreciation to Marjorie and Marian and others who helped keep Union's ministries alive during this interim. Above all, celebrate God's invitation to join together with God in the new things God is doing among us. Our goal is to be the church God wants us to be. What surprise has God for us next? We may be confident that the best is yet to come.

63

Dreams

Do things ever turn out as we expect? For example, what happened with your life? Are you today where you, as a youth, planned you'd be? Did what you are now that you're grown up turn out very different from what you wanted to be when you were growing up? Remember when you wanted to be an astronaut or a firefighter, nurse, teacher, or ...? What are you now? Are you what and where you expected to be some years ago? If so, you are a rarity. Dreams often don't come true. The "happily ever after" or the career of which you dreamed may remain only in remembered dreams, not in real life.

Does it matter whether your dreams didn't come true? Maybe, maybe not. It depends on whether the dream you had was the dream God put in your heart. If the dream was your learning to become what God meant you to be, then yes. Yes, it matters very much. If you haven't developed your God-given talents or aren't using them for the glory of God, it does matter.

In his little book *The Story of the Other Wise Man*, Henry Van Dyke depicts Artaban, a wise man who sets out to join the other magi (the ones who "made it" into the Bible) to seek the newborn King. But because Artaban isn't able to arrive at the meeting place by the designated hour, the other magi leave without him. Artaban then spends his life trying to find the One born under a star. He arrives too late at the manger in Bethlehem and too late as he pursues the holy family in Egypt. He never catches up until ... until he arrives at Golgotha ... too late, when the One whom he has sought all his life long is crucified. The sky darkens, the ground shakes, and he is dead.[3]

Artaban's dream of meeting the King appears to have come to nothing. But even as the aged magi lies dying, Christ comes to him and tells him that the good deeds he had done during his life—the times when Artaban stopped to help a needy person—have been done to the One whom Artaban sought. The acts that delayed Artaban and kept him from catching up with the star born One were services done to him. So Artaban's dream *was* fulfilled.

What about you? What about the dreams God put in your head? Do any of them still "fit" you? Do any of them still bring a sharp twinge of longing in you? Why not drag them out of yesterday, dust them off, and fulfill them tomorrow? Dreams need not die. If they are dreams God has given you to fulfill, get on with them.

I am thinking about dreams because I am remembering the dreams I had when I came to be pastor at Union a little more than two years ago. I believed my fervent prayer to God for vision of what I was called to do as your pastor, a vision of a church God wants you to become, would be fulfilled. I envisioned you as a congregation ever more open and loving, ever more earnestly seeking the lost, living ever more joyfully, trusting and intimately in relationship with God.

I won't say the dreams died or were killed. I can see that many were fulfilled—or have begun to be. I can see that we have come a long way together. Much has been accomplished. But there is still much more to be done—much God is calling Union to be and do. Listen to that call! Listen to the sweet lure of the Holy Spirit inviting you to continue to seek and serve Christ first. Listen to the gentle invitation of Christ saying, "Come, follow me. Let's go fish for people."

Listen and then do. Listen to God leading, then dare to move forward to fulfill the dreams God has given you. Soon your new pastor will be among you. It's a good time to share old dreams and dream new ones. Now is a good time to fulfill God's dream for you. Let your dreams be a bright beacon to light your tomorrow. Yes, as the poet, Langston Hughes says, "Hold fast to the dreams, for if the dreams die, life's a broken-winged bird that cannot fly."

And me? I will go with joy to serve God with a new congregation. Prayerfully, I seek to understand what God is doing in this new congregation I'm sent to serve. I plan to listen very carefully, work prayerfully, and fly on two wings, trusting that God, who has brought me this far, won't abandon me now. Thanks be to God for the goodness we have known.

64

Out of the Mouths of Robins

"I will sing of your steadfast love, O Lord, forever; with my mouth I will proclaim your faithfulness to all generations" (Psalm 89:1–2 NRSV).

I rose earlier than usual this Sunday morning. The springtime world was just too beautiful to miss. And the outdoors were noise enough to wake me. It had rained. Finally. And there was such a celebration outside that I wanted to participate. Oh, it had rained! Just enough to bring the worms up to the top of the ground. And the robins were shouting such an anthem of praise to God that they filled the air with their singing. They were not an orderly choir; their individual songs tumbled over one another with joy and enthusiasm. It seemed as if they were responding to the words of the song "Go, Tell it on the Mountains." They had no mountain, but rooftops and treetops were adequate roosts for the singers. I smiled as I thought of this "first service" music, which preceded the "second worship service" by nearly five hours. I knew the choir and congregation would be along later to add their praise and thanksgiving to God. I knew also that their enthusiasm and joy would equal and exceed that of the robins. Knoxville United Methodist Church's voice would ring out to give glory to God and joy to all who heard.

I've watched Knoxville United Methodist Church for the past four years as it has been singing praises to God and inviting the world to join in praise and worship. Results have varied. Sometimes after the most earnest and caring evangelism efforts, little response is observed. At the other times, Knoxville United Methodist Church's efforts to draw others to Christ bore fruit.

Looking back, I see a small but steady stream of folks who have come to give their lives to Christ and themselves to ministries at Knoxville United Methodist Church. Before you say, "We have no children here" or "We don't have any new people coming," look around at the new faces. Remember the large cast at the children's Christmas program. Give thanks to God.

Because of your faithfulness to the tasks God has given you, because of your caring, kind spirits, it has been an indescribable joy for Merlin and me to be in ministry with you. Thank you and keep singing! Tell it on the mountains, from the rooftops, across your back fence, everywhere! Tell of God's goodness and grace. Be positive when you speak of Knoxville United Methodist Church in the community. Imitate the robins (except for climbing the trees maybe) and let the whole world know of the joy you have found in being a Christian. Like the psalmist said, "I will praise you, O Lord, with all my heart; I will tell of all your wonders. I will be glad and rejoice in you; I will sing praises to your name, O Most High" (Psalm 9:1–2 NIV).

PART 5
Short Stories

65

Ristras

"I use rubber gloves," Caroline remarked as she slid onto the warm stones of the patio beside Marcia. "You mess with those mothers, then rub your eyes, and you've got problems—hot ones." She chuckled. Caroline took a second sip of coffee. Maria continued methodically stringing chili peppers on a strong, brown chord, seeming not to have heard.

"Yes, I know," she finally answered. Maria stretched to let the warm sun embrace her shoulders, then winced as pain reminded her of her broken ribs.

"Haven't you strung enough?" Caroline eyed the three colorful strings of peppers already hung to dry on pegs along the front of the house. "There are only two of you now, and Akira doesn't eat much chili yet."

Maria glanced at Caroline, searching the face for hostility or cruelty. She saw none, only Caroline's concerned smile. Maria sighed and turned for a quick glance at the infant sleeping on a quilt in a shaded corner of the patio. Then Maria bent her head over the basket of peppers, quickly adding one after another to the growing strand while her lips moved, but Caroline heard no sound.

"Sorry," Caroline whispered. "I hadn't meant to be cruel. The silence grew long. Caroline shifted on the stones. "You heard from him?"

Maria shook her head without lifting her eyes. They burned with tears, but she dared not wipe them with her pepper-stained fingers. The lump in her throat became heavier and burned like a good four-alarm chili. She probed the feelings as she might probe a chipped tooth, assessing the pain, the damage. She felt the burden of shame. And fear.

She shuddered, remembering her last glimpse of him staggering out the door three weeks ago, leaving her crumpled in a heap on the kitchen floor. Shame burned and something else, something new to Maria: anger.

A flicker of rage licked at her insides like the first swallow of a good salsa. Maria's hands were still over the basket of peppers as her mind replayed scene after scene of Carlos's drunken homecomings, his shoutings, his slaps and kicks, the beatings that left her broken and dazed. She tried not to remember the day after day of burning shame and fear, but they were strung in her memory like peppers on a cord, a ristra of abuse. As her mind raced over the scenes, her hands began to race to string the chili on the cord. She was jolted back to the present by Caroline's voice.

"You gonna let him come back?"

Maria felt the burning in her gut. How could she explain to the cool blonde angel seated before her? "He's my husband," Maria whispered.

"He abdicated that position, Maria! Surely you have some self-respect. You can't let him destroy you. The beatings have been worse every time. First a black eye. Now broken ribs. Next time, who knows?"

Maria bent her head over the peppers, stringing them like a nun telling her rosary. "He always says he is sorry. Maybe he will stop drinking. Akira needs a father."

Caroline pressed her face close to Maria's, forcing her to look up. "Maria, do you want Akira to grow up with memories like that of her father coming home night after night and beating on her mother? Do you want Akira to learn that that is what it means to be a woman, to be a thing for a man to vent his drunken anger upon? Maria! Think what you are doing to Akira!"

Caroline's cool voice was raised to a deep vibrating intensity that seemed to pound away at Maria's brain. Maria remembered that thudding sound and the burning in her own gut when as a child she had heard her mother's protests as her own father had beaten her. Maria remembered hiding in terror when she heard her father coming home. Remembered the voices that grew louder, sometimes ending in the screams of her mother, shouts, and curses from her father. And then the weeping. Day after day, the burning fear and shame like chili peppers strung on a cord.

"But he is my husband," Maria's mother murmured when her neighbors had gathered to console her, to persuade her that she must throw him out.

"He is your papa, Maria," Momma had said to her when Maria begged Momma to send him away.

"Is that what I am doing to Akira?" Maria whispered softly as she stared blindly into the basket of peppers.

"Well, time to break up the party," Caroline drawled. "Time to head home and fix dinner. Kids'll be home from school soon." She unwound her tall, willowy frame from her perch on the patio stones, paused until Maria had to look up. A concerned frown dented Caroline's usually serene frown. She demanded, "Maria, are you gonna be okay? You know I'm right next door if you need me." She bent impulsively, her long blonde hair flowing like a flagrant blessing on Maria's shoulders as Caroline crushed her in a brief but fierce hug. She remained crouched before Maria, staring into her eyes. "Don't give up, Maria. Don't give up on yourself, your pride, your life. Hang onto yourself." She gently placed her hand on Maria's head as if blessing her. Then she rose and strolled across the scruffy lawn toward her own front door.

Watching her, Maria found it hard to believe she had known this calm, cool bringer of hope for only a few months. Caroline was radiating a strength and assurance that she was someone of value, of worth. "I want that," Maria hissed fiercely as she stared after her friend. She wondered what that calm, self-confident femaleness of Caroline's would look like translated into Maria's idiom. *Could it be?* she wondered. *Is it possible for me? Oh, if only ...* The light began to leave her face. But her shoulders no longer sagged as she began stringing the remaining peppers into a final ristra. As she worked, she wondered what it might be like to be free of fear, free of shame, free of that nagging sense that the world would never be safe, secure that love was scarcely worth the risk.

The baby stirred and whimpered. Maria turned to the tiny face stirring into hungry wakefulness. Lifting her quickly, Maria entered the cool house. Laying Akira down, she went to scrub her hands. Free of the hot pepper juices before changing and feeding the baby, Maria inspected her face in the bathroom mirror, noting that the bruises around her eyes had faded to a sickly green. The cuts and swelling on her lips and chin were no longer very noticeable. But she noticed the eyes—the pain and distrust in her gaze— wondering whether they would fade or heal.

Later, Akira cooed contentedly in her crib in the living room as Maria returned to stringing the remaining peppers into a final ristra. Her fingers moved more slowly now as she remembered the first time she had done this task. Before the baby, before Carlos's drinking had turned her dreams into a nightmare of drunken homecomings. Before the beatings had begun, Maria's hands were still. The last pepper was strung. Her hands stung with the hot juice. As her face had stung from his first slaps, later burning with shame when Caroline had seen the bruises, the swollen lip. Maria had taken to hiding in the house, but Caroline had walked right in, sat down at the kitchen counter, waiting until Maria was ready to talk. To scream. To weep.

Maria shook herself back to the present. Leaving a generous length, she cut the needle end of the cord, on which she had strung the peppers with a sharp knife, and thrust the knife into the waistband of her skirt. Gathering the string of peppers in her cotton skirt, she climbed onto the seat of the wooden porch chair to hang the last ristra on the mesquite peg, protruding from the front of her adobe-covered home. Maria checked the knot, then flung the ristra over the peg. She arranged the glowing peppers in the fading light, stretching on tip toe to reach those nearest the high peg.

Suddenly she felt something grab her at mid-thigh in a strong grasp. Maria screamed, grabbed the mesquite peg in one hand. She kicked in terror and turned to see Carlos grinning his drunken smirk. Maria froze for an instant in fear as the reek of sweat and booze stung her nostrils. Then she took a deep breath and commanded in a voice of steadiness and strength that surprised them both, "Take your hands off me, Carlos."

"Hi, baby." Carlos murmured, snuggling his face into her calico-covered crotch.

Maria's scream had awakened the sleeping baby, who began to wail in fear. "Carlos, I must see to Akira," Maria commanded. He let her go so abruptly that she grasped for the mesquite peg to keep from plunging to the stone patio floor beneath her. As she swayed for a long moment in midair, clutching the rough peg and struggling to find the seat of the wooden chair with her feet, she heard Carlos tumbling into the house. Just as her feet finally found the chair, she heard Carlos's shouts and a crash, followed by Akira's screams.

"My baby!" Maria cried as she jumped down from the chair. She was startled to see that she had grasped the pod of a chili pepper off the ristra as she fell. Its flesh was dripping in the center of the living room. A table and lamp were overturned. Akira's blankets were flung in a lumpy pile against the fireplace wall. In the midst of the blankets, an outraged Akira, bleeding from the cut on her forehead, thrashed about, screaming.

"Shut her up, or I will," Carlos threatened as he lurched toward the kitchen. As Maria knelt to take up her child, she heard the refrigerator door open, the snap of a pull tab torn from the top of a beer can. "Come here, baby," Carlos commanded, coming to stand in the living room. He loomed in the doorway, blocking escape. She stood, no longer terrified, now only enraged and watchful. She wouldn't be a victim again. As Carlos moved toward her, Maria shifted Akira into her left arm. As Carlos swayed forward to clutch at her, her hand moved swiftly to brush the dripping red pepper flesh across his eyes. Carlos screamed in agony as the hot juices seared. He lashed out in rage and confusion, but Maria was already out the door, bound for freedom.

"You and me, we're going to be okay," she crooned soothingly to the whimpering child. The strength was still in her voice.

66

Stained Glass

Crystal's pen slashed across the large sheet of drawing paper with deft, sure stokes. A design evolved. She held it at arm's length, studying it intently. Dropping the drawing, she gulped from a mug of strong coffee, stretched, then scrunched down into the padded kitchen chair and closed her eyes. *Best way I know to avoid postpartum depression*, she thought, remembering with pleasure the work just completed. Early this morning, she had supervised the hanging of a multi-paneled work. When the elegant art lovers had gathered later in the newly restored mansion, the spring sun poured through the intricate stained-glass designs of Crystal's latest creation and evoked appreciative silences and sounds. The gallery had been packed, but Crystal had by choice slipped unknown among the gallery goers, glowing as brightly as her work to hear the admiration it evoked. What an ego trip!

Still smiling, Crystal returned to the new drawing. But the kitchen clock caught her eye. *It's time … quarter till five!* She had tensed and half risen, a look of fear and dismay sweeping her face before she remembered: *Poppa's not coming home.*

A child sat alone at the kitchen table; feet curled around the chrome ledge of a battered vinyl-covered chair. Books and school papers strewn across the table were ignored as she solemnly moved fragments of broken colored glass about. She arranged and rearranged until satisfied with the design. Shapes of various shades of green soda bottles mingled with the browns of beer bottles. Central was her prize, a triangle of blue milk of magnesia container found minutes before on the dusty walk home from school. She had just lifted three of the carefully juxtaposed shapes to let the afternoon light gleam through.

The slender girl stiffened, glancing at the clock as she gathered glass, books, and papers and scooted up the narrow stairs to her loft bedroom. Slamming the door against the image of the quarter-till-five clock face, she huddled on the bed and rocked, weeping very softly.

"Crystal, ya'll come down here and set the table. Your poppa be home soon. You know he gits right fussy if'n his supper ain't ready."

Silence.

"Crystal? Crystal, you git yourself down here."

The child slid off the bed and picked her way slowly down the stairs. Silently, she began to place chipped plates and mismatched silver on the faded tablecloth. At the sound of an approaching vehicle, her pace quickened. Finishing her task, she again darted for the stairs.

"Crystal, where you goin'? Don't you hear Poppa's truck? Come her 'n' stir the gravy while I slice the meat."

The child crept to the range, seeming to diminish into as small a bundle of humanity as possible. The hand lifting the wooden spoon trembled.

A truck stopped with a last rattle of the loose front bumper. A truck door slammed. Heavy boots beat on the wooden porch floor. Dust disturbed by the truck wheels and a whining hound drifted into the room before him. He stood, blinking in the dim light.

"Hey," the woman called softly in greeting.

"Supper ready?" He dropped heavily into the chair from which Crystal had recently fled.

"Crystal, ain't you gonna give Poppa a kiss?" Momma ordered.

The girl shrank, and the spoon stilled. She stood there, silent, mouth tight.

Poppa turned, heavy brows glowering, hand stirring his greasy black hair. His flashy lips grinned crookedly as he winked knowingly at the child. "Ain't you gonna give Poppa a kiss," he growled mockingly.

The child paled visibly, tensed, and seemed to vibrate like an over-tuned instrument.

"Crystal, what am I gonna do with you?" Momma snapped as she wiped her hands on her worn apron. "This here's the only poppa you ever gonna have. He's tryin' to do right by us. How you ..."

The shrill voice trailed off to a sullen whine as the face of the girl closed and the light went out behind her gray eyes. Momma's eyes stared in horror as Crystal's glance flared with naked hatred. They dimmed then with an empty look as if a house when the lights are switched off. Momma shivered. "It's not normal, a little girl don't love her daddy. Crystal, the devil's got ahold of you for sure!"

Crystal fled. Behind the closed door of her little room, she could hear only a faint murmur of voices. Rocking, weeping. She stared at the cracked ceiling.

She walked with as little movement as possible, trying to silence the deafening rustle of the hand-me-down taffeta dress. She slipped into the pew, bare thighs squeaking on the darkly stained wood as she slid to the very end. She pressed herself as far as possible from Poppa.

The preacher thundered, raged. Crystal sought to deafen, blind herself to the judgmental tone, the accusing figure.

"Evil women, tempting good men into sin ... whereas ... Temptresses with painted faces and wanton eyes ... The devil walks among us ... Scarlet women ..."

Crystal kept her eyes lowered and focused her entire strength on stilling the whisper that rose in her throat.

"Be sure your sin will find you out. God knows what is in your heart!"

With relief, Crystal heard the ancient organ wheeze into the first words, which stuck in her throat as the congregation sang, "There is a fountain filled with blood ... And sinners, plunged beneath that flood, lose all their guilty stain, lose all their guilty stains."

Guilty ... guilty ... stains ... stains ...

A gust of rough April breeze stirred the new design. Light from the afternoon sun glowed through the small stained-glass work hanging in the window before her. Crimson, blue, and gold lights flecked the table drawing paper. Crystal thrust out her hand so the dancing flickers of color hued her hand scarlet, amber, blue. "Stained glass," she murmured, more weariness than bitterness coloring her voice.

She studied the hanging artistry, smaller than a panel, larger than a suncatcher. It was skewed, as if a clumsy hand had dropped it on its lower left-hand corner. An accidentally unsymmetrical cross rose above a muddy blue sky. An angel lurked precariously above what might have been the dark hole of a cave. A figure knelt nearby. Blobs of extra lead obscured cut edges, filling in the interstices with opaque dullness.

Crystal smiled at the clumsiness of this first effort. Her mind drifted through the faces of clients who displayed her later work in homes, offices, and galleries. "What would they think of you?" she whispered softly to the angel. "But everybody needs a guardian angel, I guess mine just came too late."

He lunged at her, a strangeness in his eyes. She struggled against his massive arms, turning from his fetid whiskey breath. She struggled until subdued by the sheer mass of him. Flight and breath were blocked. Clothes, then flesh were torn. Pain and then darkness came.

She awoke alone, bleeding. The whimpering animal sounds were her own. She lay for what seemed hours in the darkness, dazed. Stunned. Later, she struggled to rise; heavily she moved. Cleaned herself. Hid stained linens, ruined clothing. Then she dozed fitfully. Dreams drove her screaming out of sleep, and she awoke to his face looming darkly over her.

"You tell your momma I'll kill you." She hiccupped and reeled away. "You tease," he growled, lurching out the door. Crystal crept into the darkened sanctuary. The stillness was noisy with rustlings and creaks, of presence and memories. She slipped into the pew farthest from where they usually sat during worship. She moved as one who feels fragile or already broken for a long time; she hunched over herself, clenched fists knotted in her lap, head bowed. The sun burst forth through the rushing clouds, and the full light of the day broke through the stained-glass windows, flooding the church with a kaleidoscope of color. She studied the intricate patterns of each window, rapt.

Finally, she breathed deeply and glanced down at her hands, which were folded loosely in her lap. Restrained light fell on her hands, bathing them in color. Crystal flinched as if burned, clambered hastily out of the pew, and fled.

An angry rush of wind tossed debris and the first sprinkles of a spring rain against the kitchen window, setting the askew stained-glass panel clinking against the window glass. Crystal rose to still the wobbly angel, which veered in the wind as if in desperate need of flying instruction.

She ran her finger gently across the cool surface of the glass. "Hang on, Gabriel," she murmured, smiling at the clumsy appearance. She studied the face of the bent figure beneath with a solemn security. The clumsiness of the artist had given the kneeling woman's face a twisted, bitter expression, a ghost of that which she had once worn. "Hang on," she whispered, this time to herself and the self she had been.

A small workshop with sheets of colored glass and tools were strewn on workbench, counters, and table. Blobs of lead, acrid scents of acid and heated metal. Crystal hunched over her worktable with sweat and tears falling onto the surface of her first work. She lifted her head and stepped back to study the finished panel. With mingled shame and rage, she glared at the lifeless work lying like some lumpish dead creature before her. She eyed the hammer briefly, then lifted the stained glass and lead thing without looking at it. As she turned to place it in the farthest corner, the sun caught for a moment the object in her hands; the dead thing flickered into life, then died. Crystal didn't notice.

Yet she worked, fitting, cutting, shaping, assembling: the work healing, the quiet solitude safe. Occasionally, a subtle radiance lit her eyes as the joy of creation drove the shadows from them. There was no peace, but sometimes enough weariness came to permit sleep, to banish dreams.

Once ... only once Poppa had intruded. She had been lifting a sheet of glass to the streaming light in a blessing-seeking gesture, studying the graining for cloud shapes. The color suffused her face, making it seem to glow from within. She turned. Poppa stood in the doorway of her sanctuary. A look of almost wonder touched his eyes. A heavy hand lifted as if to touch an intricate hanging, newly completed, then jerked back as if burned. He had fled as if demon pursued from among the sacred symbols. The perpetual sneer was absent from his face.

Crystal had closed the door then for the first and only time upon her sanctuary. Quickly she stacked the newly completed work with a host of others, leaned overlapping along the longest wall of her shop in the chronology of their creation. She began again at once, working feverishly, compulsively, furiously far into the night. Once Momma had come and stood in the doorway, watching silently for a long time.

Then: "Bedtime, Crystal? Aren't you tired, girl?"

"No, Momma, I'll finish this."

By morning another work lay on the workbench. When she lifted it against the east window, it blazed in the morning sun. Crimson and scarlet shades of glass glowed as with fire. A wild configuration in glass set every surface afire with color. For a moment only. Then a stone-faced Crystal stacked it with the others against the far wall.

Those had been hard years, compulsive years, driven years, years of striving to do, to do well, to be better. Years of striving to exorcize the demon, to find meaning, rest, to drive away the dreams.

Strobe lights flashing, pulsing, crimson, blue, amber, Poppa's face looming. Crystal running, straining in soundless screams. Faces melting and reforming. Gabriel, the annunciation, silent. No subtitles.

Crystal worked, shaking, tangled, sweating, throat dry from unborn screams. She leaped from the bed and raced to her workshop to sit on her high stool until the thudding of her heart eased and the first light of dawn winked through the window to fall on the floor before her.

Poppa is gone. Poppa is gone. The litany began to bring calm. Haunted eyes turned unseeing toward morning.

She'd learned the litany to bring sleep, as some count sheep, for the rage had begun to burn in her with such heat that even the work in her shop didn't bring release. Dream-haunted nights drove her back to the workshop, but her hands lay idle in her lap. She sat still, weary, until exhaustion at dawn made a little rest possible. *You can't hang on much longer,* she had warned herself. That was when the voice had come to help her.

Crystal flipped unseeing through the pages of a three-year-old *Psychology Today* in the reception area of her gynecologist's office. Tired and tense from her efforts to still the mounting anxiety with which she faced her second pelvic exam, Crystal had grabbed the only periodical in sight. "Talking Yourself Out of Anxiety." The title caught her eye. Barely able to concentrate at first, she gradually began to focus on the article's content. Supposedly, if you talked to yourself and worked systematically to relax periodically, you could reduce symptoms of anxiety and survive stressful situations. *It's worth a try,* she thought, remembering with embarrassment the previous year when she had hyperventilated before her first pelvic exam.

So Crystal talked to herself. The voice was born. The rational, cool voice that had known the secret source of her anxiety became a friend. Naming the fear she had been unable to name, she intoned, "It's not Poppa. Relax. It's not Poppa; relax."

By the time Dr. Hall's nurse had motioned her into the examining room that day, the voice had calmed her. *It works,* she thought. The litany had sustained her through the years. It was strengthened by a workshop in self-hypnosis at the local junior college. Crystal was beginning to take charge of her life. With the voice she learned to sleep. As some counted sheep, popped pills, made love, Crystal had her voice.

The telephone shrilled her out of sleep. Momma's voice: "Crystal, Poppa's dyin'. You come home."

Creeping into the dim room where the once-puffy-puffy face lay cadaverous on the pillow. The voice: *Relax. Be not afraid.*

The once-terrifying eyes flickered open, steadied, held. Was it fear that lit them? Was even Poppa frightened?

"Poppa, Crystal's here. Poppa, Crystal's come home."

The once-terrifying eyes flickered open, steadied, held.

Was it fear that had lit them? Was even Poppa afraid?

Momma slipped away to fetch a cool cloth for his feverish forehead. Crystal moved closer, growing calmer, determined.

"Poppa …" His harsh breathing caught and held for a moment. "Poppa, I … forgive you." Crystal's eyes burned with an intensity that drove the other gaze to falter, drop. His eyes misted. What might have been a tear slid down on a life-roughed cheek, its trail catching the evening light like a comet tail. Thus, did Lucifer fall like a burning brand from heaven. The eyes closed.

"He's gone," Momma whispered. "It's Poppa's time, I reckon."

Poppa's time. Poppa's time. Time for Poppa to come home.

He stood like an angel in the pulpit, light breaking through the rose window to fall on him. His eyes roved, boring with intensity, engaging those of His congregation. Behind the excitement of his voice was an almost chuckle as of some glad secret were about to bubble out. On this, the new minister's first Sunday, Crystal had scarcely lifted her eyes, sneaking no more than an occasional quick, shy glimpse.

"In the name of Jesus Christ, your sins are forgiven," he proclaimed. And the resonant baritone struck a shiver down Crystal's neck. Her eyes lighted, lifted, locked on him. "God loves you. God love you," he exulted. Crystal blushed, and her eyes remained on the shimmer of crimson light hovering on her tightly clutched hands. The summer sun set the windows aflame. Her hands unclenched in a gesture of receiving. The light played on her upturned palms.

"The Light of the World is Jesus," the choir rejoiced, as if they, too, had grasped the glad news Rev. Gabriel had pronounced.

"Anybody home?" The voice, full of thinly veiled laughter, floated through the open door of her workroom and startled her from her reveries. Crystal jumped up, smoothing her hair and rumpled khaki shorts with nervous gestures. Shocked speechless by his sudden appearance, she stood stiffly, peering into his eyes.

"Hello. Did I come in at a bad time? I was calling in the neighborhood, and I thought I would catch you while you were home. I ..."

Her absolute rigidity, her pale and strained face stopped his smile, his voice. He stood uncertainly in the doorway, as one who discovers some wild creature and freezes lest it run away.

The struggle in her face ended with a slight loosening of its tension. "Hello. You, uh ... startled me," she responded softly. "I ..." She lowered her eyes and bowed her head weekly, intent on some internal dialogue.

"May I sit down, or ..." A puzzled note had crept into his voice, matching the glance, which searched her face, seeking some clue, some explanation for her dismayed response. This wasn't the woman whose bright face responded to his messages about God's love with increasing warmth and joy. *He is not Poppa. He is not Poppa*, the reasonable, calm voice intoned. With the repetition of the litany, color began to return to her cheeks. The light went on again behind her eyes, and a smile flicked the corner of her mouth. But the eyes didn't remain on his.

"Tea?"

"Yes, thanks."

Crystal turned quickly to fill her hot pot with water and plug it in. She caught quick glimpses of him beneath her lowered lashes as she placed tea into a ceramic pot and pulled two bags from a rack on the wall. *He is not Poppa. He is not Poppa*, the calm, dispassionate voice reassured. Gradually her movements slowed; the trembling of her hands ceased.

"You ... uh, you're an artist? You work with stained glass?" His eyes roved her workroom with open curiosity as his laughter-bubbling voice washed over her.

She eyed him sharply but saw no mocking, no judgment, in his face. "No, I ... Yes, I ... Sugar?"

"What? Oh, no thanks."

Made nervous again by his scrutiny of her sanctuary, she quickly poured the tea and set the steaming mugs on a tray. Heading purposefully toward the doorway, she called, "Let's go into the living room."

"No. Please, let's stay here. I'll only stay a moment. I see I've interrupted your work, and I don't want to keep you from ..." The glance roved about the room, locked on the work leaning against the wall.

Crystal flushed, sought small talk, but in her tension no words would come. Finally: "I, that is, it's not my work. I just ..." Her eyes sought his, held, seeking answers to questions she hadn't asked, didn't know.

"May I see?" He rose quickly and grasped the just-finished panel, raising it powerfully toward the south light. He stood, arms uplifted, head thrown back, face intent. A look of pleasure stirred his face. She had seen him thus when he lifted the chalice for blessing, light from the stained-glass altar wall falling on him, but the radiance seeming to come from within him.

"You did this?" His eyes were searching hers, incredulous, "I had no idea you were so gifted. I mean, this is incredible." Gently, reverently, he began to lift the panels ranged along the wall one by one, holding them to the light, studying them intently, and then laying them gently aside. He worked methodically, nodding occasionally, smiling, silent.

Crystal had shrunk into a bundle of shame and confusion, face twisted by some struggle, tension increasing with each panel. Finally, as he reached for one of the last works, her voice rasped out, "Stop!"

He turned, registering surprise as if he had forgotten her presence. He frowned at her tone, her tension.

"Please." She could trust her voice no longer. Exposed, violated, ashamed, she clutched the tea mug and bent over it as if thirsty.

"What's wrong? Have I upset you?"

Silence.

"Crystal, this work is beautiful. You are a talented artist. But of course you know that. I'm sorry I sound so surprised, but I had never heard of anyone speak of your work. I had no idea ..."

She made no response. He paused, looking at her bowed head. "Crystal? Crystal?" He came to stand before her, but she didn't move or answer. Finally, softly, he said, "I don't understand. Would you like me to go away?"

The voice, louder than his, screamed, *This is not the same. This is not Poppa. Relax. This is not Poppa. Let him come in.*

"Crystal, I have no idea what I've done to upset you, but I must leave to make a hospital call. I'll stop by later this afternoon to see if you are all right."

She nodded without looking up. Soon she heard the outside door to her studio latch softly behind him. When he had gone, she stood for some moments, head bent, breathing quickly as if she had just finished a race. She struggled to restore order to her thoughts. Finally, she raised her head and looked around her studio in surprise and shock. She had expected devastation, destruction, as if some enemy had invaded, bombed, laid waste. The room appeared unchanged except that the panels of stained glass, which had leaned along the wall, were now propped along the sills of the large studio windows. She was stunned. There was beauty. The room was rainbowed by their hues. Color danced on walls, floor, and every surface. Intricate patterns, finely detailed, transformed the plain glass walls. Crystal stood enchanted, rapt, afraid to breathe, lest they shatter. She noticed another change in the room: it was empty without him.

And the terse voice intoned, *He wasn't Poppa. He wasn't Poppa.* The voice trailed off. Crystal smiled, wept, and laughed aloud.

She stared through the kitchen window, enjoying the spring flowers and newly greening grass. The world was larger. She moved to slide the glass patio doors open and to gulp the hyacinth-scented air. The stained-glass panel shivered in the slight breeze, but Crystal turned her back on her guardian angel, slipped off her shoes, and tossed them aside.

The interview had gone well. After the first curious sizing up, her few questions had been quick and nervous. Crystal felt silly pretending that facts mattered. Libra, the girl had blushed. Cheerfully: "Yes, that's my name. My mother was a hippie!"

Libra had unwrapped the brown paper covering the flat, heavy parcel and looked expectantly at Crystal. There were both shyness and pride in the glances. Moved, Crystal forced herself to examine technique dispassionately. Smooth cuts, even metal work. She would do. Taking a deep breath, Crystal called out, "Come."

Libra's face became animated; then she stepped to the exact center of the room. She studied each work of glass, each piece of raw material, each tool, each dent or scar on the work surfaces, turning a few degrees at a time and studying each new vista. When she had gone full circle, she gazed gracefully into Crystal's eyes. "I could be happy here," she stated flatly.

The corner of Crystal's mouth twitched into the beginning of a smile. I could be happy with this assistant. It is time. It was time to let someone in.

Passing through the kitchen on her way out, the girl had looked curiously at the oddly skewed panel in the window. She studied the piece with the clumsy, hovering angel and turned with a question in her eyes.

Crystal laughed. "My guardian angel, the first piece I ever did. I was quite young. I … a teacher took an interest in my work at school, thought I had talent, called my grandmother, who was a friend of hers. Grandma set my studio up in the solarium and … well, here I am!" She shrugged and chuckled.

The warm air was soft, fragrant with new grass. The carpet of green tickled her winter-tendered feet. She loosed the combs that held her long hair and let it fall softly about her shoulders. Stretching her arms up toward the warm sun, Crystal felt whole, happy, healed. A noise. She started and started and whirled toward the open doorway.

Gabriel leaned against the doorjamb, the sun setting fire to his blond hair and his head and arms. Crystal caught her breath and turned to glimpse the askew glass angel. Its light was gone. Crystal's stiffness had also vanished. Gabe came often to watch her work, to watch her. Hair glowing and eyes alight with that strange inner radiance, she approached him and leaned surely against warm length.

Later, she would remember and smile. "I forgot to say, 'It's not Poppa.'"

67

Final Effects

"I said never come back," P.J. whispered slowing the car only enough to negotiate the sharp turn from the main road to a winding tree-lined lane. Red dust hung like a pall in her wake and seemed to shimmer before her eyes.

Home. The word hung in her mind like the reverberations from the sounding of a great gong. Home? She felt tension mounting, choking off breath and knotting her stomach. Home. *I'd never come back to this twisted, destroying world, I said.* The line of spring-flowering trees, each planted to commemorate a special occasion in the life of what had once been a family, blurred by on either side. She would not glance at them, especially "her" tree, the one her father had planted the day Priscilla Jayne had been born. Even the thought of its crooked trunk added to the boil of feelings within her. She was aware of rage and hurt emerging along with a sense of alienation, of not belonging here, of having been rejected and banished. She forgot to maintain calm, trying for a sense of disengagement. *I'll finish this in a hurry,* she thought as she braked roughly to a stop before the stately white-columned house. But she caught her breath as a powerful flow of nostalgia swept away the calm, and a wistful yearning struck her like a wave of nausea. "I'm a fool," she muttered to the dusty air, starting at the sightless lower windows as if daring the mansion to evoke tears from her.

She stormed up the worn stairs, thrust the key harshly into the lock, and pushed the heavy door open with such force that it thudded against the wall. Her father stared at her. Appraising, cold gray eyes peered down at her from the portrait on the wall. Just so had he had looked at her twenty years ago when she left for boarding school.

Then P. J. had stood in the middle of the large front hall, numerous pieces of luggage reflected in the polished gleam of the floor. Her father had roared as Mother and servants rushed about with last-minute preparations.

"Lily, can't you do anything right? The train leaves in fifteen minutes. I told you to have that girl ready by nine o'clock."

"That girl" stood silent, wretched, seething with rage as the servants brought in the last of her things. Then her mother, taking her place just behind her father, said softly, "She's ready." Mother straightened to her full height and turned toward P. J. She remembered that look—that strange mixture of appeal and triumph—and remembered returning it with the most forbidding look she could muster with her fourteen-year-old face. She wouldn't betray the sense of abject terror that threatened to send her screaming upstairs to her room.

But she had submitted—as a lamb before the shearers is silent—remembering all the way to the station that look on her mother's face and her own rage. Betrayed by her own mother! Why had Mother not defended her? Why had she never said P. J. was acceptable as she was? Why had she permitted Father to send P. J. to be molded into one of those weak, ineffectual porcelain dolls like her mother? How dare they think she'd let them make a lady of her at boarding school! Thus, she had left, vowing never to return to this once home from whence she had been cast out.

P. J. shook herself from her reverie, and, lifting down Father's portrait in the heavy gilt frame from its place in the hall, she turned it to face the wall. "There, that's what I think of Miz Lily's final effects. But I must hurry. I still have things to do in town," P. J. reminded herself aloud as if her voice would keep whatever memories lurked here at bay.

She would return toward evening to freshen up before greeting the folk who would come to pay their last respects to "Miz Lily" Haymer. P. J. smiled as she remembered the solemn face of the mortician as they had completed funeral arrangements. "You'll be wanting to go on out to the home place to make arrangements for Miz Lily's final effects, I suppose," he had intoned mournfully. P. J. had been so amused by his heavy solemnity that she looked quickly down to hide her smile, only to feel a chuckle rising as she saw the obsequious kneading of his trimly manicured hands.

She fled then, before totally disgracing herself and the Haymer name, of course, by her hysterical laughter.

The smile fled from P. J.'s face as she recalled the pale face of her mother. What was that look on her mother's face when P. J., summoned to her dying mother's bedside by the family doctor, had entered the hospital room? Had the look held triumph? P. J. knew only that she had been taken aback at the strength of that gaze and the grip of her mother's soft hand; it was hard to believe she had been dying in that first moment, yet with P. J.'s arrival, the strength fled like air from a punctured balloon. Within minutes, she seemed withered and frail. Yet within those minutes, Mother had looked silently long, hard, and earnestly at P. J. as if to memorize her face to take with her. There had been something wonderfully complete, satisfied, self-assured, and strong in the gaze of the frail woman, whom P. J. had come to think of as weak, ineffectual, useless.

"Enough of this! I'll never finish with … Miz Lily's last effects at this rate," she muttered to the silent house. P. J. quickly climbed the winding staircase, hand caressing the polished banister, down which she had taken many furtive slides before being caught by her father and whipped brutally. "I'll not have you behave yourself like white trash. You are a Haymer, and we will have none of that from a Haymer lady."

Mother had stood there, just out of Father's view, seeing P. J.'s shame, the porcelain profile drawn taut with anger. It occurred to P. J. for the first time to ask, At whom was Mother angry? P.J.'s feet made no sound on the faded, thick carpeting as she topped the stairs and opened the first door on the right. Mother's place. *Mother's place*, P. J. mused. *Now why did I call it "Mother's place?"* she wondered as she looked around the dim room. The effect was softness, fragility, restrained opulence, unreality of wasted silk, and ruffles and lace and lavender—smothering softness … the fragrance of lavender everywhere. P. J. stood in the doorway, kept from entering by an emerging memory … a garden party, guests clustered about the lawn, gardens, and verandahs. Music from a small orchestra, punch bowls and elegant sandwiches and pastries. And Mother, a fragile porcelain figure in ruffles and lace, emanating soft clouds of lavender fragrance. Mother arguing theology with an embarrassed clergyman, who seemed to be seeking an escape as guests looked on with amused smirks and disapproving glances. Then Father glided almost silently to Mother's side and hissed in that terrifyingly threatening way, "Lily Haymer, remember your place."

P. J. remembered still how Father's shadow had loomed so large and so suddenly over her where she had stood while listening with fascination as Mother had articulated some obscure point, her face animated by the excitement of debate. P. J., enraptured by the power and authority with which Mother had been speaking, was caught momentarily off her guard and paralyzed by the sudden eclipsing of her own shadow beneath Father's looming shade. Even now she could remember her fear, the scent of apple blossoms and Mother's lavender, and her puzzlement. Why did Father want Mother to remember this room? P. J. smiled sadly at her child's innocence and misunderstanding.

She took a few steps into the room and again drank in the scent of lavender. Mother's place, sanctum sanctorum, a safe house against the tight-lipped rage of her father, which, finding no response in her mother, could so quickly spill over onto P. J. or any other object within range. But what had happened to turn Mother's place from safe house to place of betrayal? *How was it that I never felt here that she was ashamed of me?* P. J. wondered. *Not once did I imagine that the lovely Lily was ashamed of her high-spirited, question-asking daughter. Why did I never guess that she believed that what I was, was unacceptable?* Then the sudden betrayal ...

P. J. felt a momentary dizziness and slumped into her mother's rocker. From this perch she often looked out on the formal gardens below. Now she leaned her head against the polished mahogany chair back and closed her eyes, rocking gently. How many hours had she spent here, rocked in mother's arms, cuddled, listening to her mother's soft, but too-clipped-for-the-south voice spinning endless, wonderful stories. There had been stories from the Bible.

No! P. J. jerked upright, her eyes wide open. No! Not stories from the Bible. Not exactly ... but where? P. J. was puzzled. Had she almost forgotten? She lifted her mother's worn Bible from the chairside table. It fell open to a sheaf of yellowed papers. Gently she unfolded them: "The Story of Deborah," "Miriam," "Mary and Martha," "How the Goddess Created the World." The age-crisped pages contained story after story after rewritten story of Bible characters. Each was the story of a woman, a heroine, a strong, triumphant person. In her mother's faded, spidery hand was her own cannon. But why? Why rewrite these stories? Why envision God as a woman? The final page was a list of scripture citations. Its faded writing listed passages portraying God as living, forgiving, nurturing mothering. Why?

Puzzled, P. J. leaned back and closed her eyes, remembering how

Mother had rocked away childhood afternoons, sharing stories of her days as an educator, a classroom teacher, as the principal of a school in the North. How she had met Father on one of his many business trips to the North, how he had seemed to love her high-spirited, intelligent spunk, how ... P. J. jolted back through what she had just been telling herself. Was that right? Mother strong? Mother telling of her business adventures, her administrative acumen. Yes. But Mother? My weak, ineffectual, porcelain mother? But was she? Could I have put the truth of her strength away for so long that it was almost lost? But the betrayal, that certainly was truth!

The words of the psalm by which P. J. had come to survive rang in her ears, "When my father and mother forsake me, then the Lord will take me up." Had the betrayal not been true? Had she not been forsaken? Had she been given up to God for ... The image of a faithful mother bringing her small child to the temple to be trained in the service of God floated into P. J.'s mind. Could it be? P. J. struggled to remember and to not remember, to block the flood of undammed memories that suddenly wouldn't be stopped. Each story had been an encouragement to become strong, independent, and resourceful. P. J.'s mind could scarcely grasp it. Strong like Mother! Each story had been an affirmation of gifts and graces, a celebration, giving the sense of one's connectedness beyond the self, beyond this room, beyond the long row of trees.

It couldn't be. P. J. rose restlessly from the chair and wandered among the delicate furniture to stand breathlessly beside another window. The early spring view was enchanting as flowering redbud, dogwood, apple, and cherry trees spread out beneath and before her toward the main road. She struggled to open the window and let the scent of blossoming trees fill the room. She had played as a child among those trees with ... whom? Mother? Her regal, stately posed mother playing? Who else? Maggie? Yes, it was Maggie, the maid in her black-and-white uniform, her black face gleaming with sweat and a smile. And Charmaine and Johnboy and Rachel, white eyes and teeth gleaming in dark faces. *We were playing during a break from lessons.* Could that be? *Yes, surely Mother had given us all lessons in the parlor while Father was away on business. And we had broken bread together, all with an excitement and a sense of tension as we engaged in those illicit activities together.* But there was more: a sense of freedom, a drunkenness born of rebellion and new life.

But that day we had been playing tag among the flowering trees, in celebration of life and spring and freedom and fellowship and learning. *Drunk with it all, we had run and danced, kicking up the red Carolina dirt until it clung in the soft haze among the trees and dusted our sweaty bodies and clothes. We were giggling and puffing as we ran, and I was running backward, laughing, until I saw faces of Johnboy and Rachel crumple, their eyes flash before being cast down, their bodies shrink and shrivel into abject postures in an instant before I thudded into something soft. Looking up, I saw Father glaring at me with such rage that I thought I would surely die on the spot. And Father screamed his racial remarks, and "Lily, you're a Haymer! You trying to start trouble? Remember your place" roaring after me as I fled.*

For years that scene had haunted P. J., even when she had been sent to the North, even after finishing school and college and seminary, even in the first parish, where the dark, fear-struck face of a child, the submissive posture of an adult, could evoke that scene of her father's rage, her mother's silent submission to the tongue lashing, and P. J.'s own running, running, running, panting, and clawing up the stairs to hide in Mother's room.

So that's where that comes from, P. J. mused. Only one other image had been such a powerful and constant companion. She had come to school late following a dental appointment. Shouts and laughter informed her that recess was in progress. As she hastened around the dark-red building, the shouts grew louder, becoming mixed with hostile cries. Rounding the corner, P. J. saw an excited ring of students, almost obscuring the two struggling in the center.

Both words and sight caught her in a double blow.

"Kill 'em, Perry."

"Don't let that bully getcha down."

"Hit 'em, Perry."

Her favorite cousin, Perry Haymer, lay on the ground, the knees of the largest eighth-grader, Jimmy Lee Stonebraker, pinning him into the dust. P. J. dropped her books and somehow catapulted herself through the tight knot of animated observers. Powered by some unknown strength, she leaped on the back of Jimmy Lee, who continued to pummel Perry's paler face. P. J.'s fingers twisted into Jimmy Lee's hair, yanking back with such sudden force that he yowled and tumbled backward. P. J. turned to help the surprised Perry to his feet, but his already-red face flushed a deeper shade, and he pulled away angrily. Her overture rejected, P. J. turned toward her friends and became aware that the laughter and taunts were now directed toward her. The huddled ring of students parted to let her pass. She looked into the faces of friends, seeing face after face closed, contorted by hostility, anger, condemnation.

P. J. didn't understand. She turned again to Perry, expecting camaraderie, warmth, but he pulled away, muttering, "Git away from me. What's the matter with you? Ain't you made enough trouble?" P. J. spent the rest of the school day alone, avoided by the other students. She caught them looking curiously or disapprovingly at her, whispering and giggling, but she endured. When the final bell rang and she could escape, she picked up her books and wearily trudged to the spot where the Haymer black sedan always waited for her. Willy, Father's driver, seeing her solemn face, silently opened the rear door and closed it behind her. For the first time P. J. didn't glance wistfully at the row of yellow buses, where the other children noisily gathered for the trip home. Today for the first time P. J. didn't resent Father's statement, "Haymers do not ride school buses." Today P. J. was grateful to enter the car's cool interior and shut out the whispers, taunts, and jeers of her classmates and to escape their icy stares or turned backs.

P. J. still didn't understand, as the car pulled into the tree-lined lane, what taboo she had broken, what wrong she had committed to so enrage her peers. But already a new thought struck her: whatever had caused her sudden ostracism, would it also set off Father's anger? P. J. shuddered. Trying to regain control of her thoughts and to deal strictly with the business at hand, P. J. started the old ritual of counting the trees in the long-curved row that ran from the main road to Circle Drive. Naming the trees, beginning with the first, which Father had ordered planted when he brought his beautiful bride home from the North, had been a favorite ploy to calm the racing of her heart when she had sought sanctuary in Mother's place. At least it had been a favorite pastime until … until the shame had started. Her tree was crooked, distorted, tied into some semblance of uprightness by stakes and guy wires attached to a thick collar around the trunk. The tree had seemed a paradigm of all P. J. found wrong with herself. So she couldn't endure the long drive from school without a sense of deep shame. P. J. took to looking the other way, pretending one of the other trees was her tree, hoping a sudden summer storm might tear her crooked tree out by the roots. But her tree had remained, one of the last things she had seen as her father hauled her away to the train that would take her to "finishing school." The tree had had the last say, bearing public witness to her clumsiness, her grotesque self, which neither bras, braces, ruffles, laces, perfumes, paternal anger, peer shunning, or anything else anyone had devised could turn into an acceptable personage before her father's disapproving gaze.

P. J. took a breath and looked down at her tree. But where was it? She counted carefully, looked again. But there was no misshapen tree in the long line. Where her tree should have been was only another normal tree, much like all the others. They must have bulldozed it out and replaced it with a perfect tree in her absence, just as they had rooted her out of home and replaced her with ... what? What had her mother done to pass her lonely days? P. J.'s eyes strayed, searching for some possible diversion. The walls of the sitting area of Mother's large room was lined with bookshelves, P. J. was startled to realize. They had always been here, a part of the furnishings, but had no special significance to her as a child. Now P. J. drew near to really look at the spines, noting philosophy, theology, science, economics, literature, the inspiration and wisdom of the ages behind delicate lead-paned glass doors. *Is this how my mother spent the long days of her life, reading and thinking, hidden away from Father's displeasure in her place at last?*

P. J. noted with pleasure the beautiful leather bindings, a collection of gold-leafed titles. Some were rare; others were fine and tastefully bound. But in one corner behind a silk-covered chaise lounge was a long row of inexpensive composition books in paper bindings, the green and white mottled covers, a striking contrast to the rest of the collection. Puzzled, P. J. pulled out one at random, opening it with curiosity. It was a journal. She pulled another and another, finding year after year of journal entries in her mother's beautiful hand. "I wonder," P. J. murmured to the silent room, "what mother wrote the day I was sent away." Quickly, she thumbed through the journals until she located the year, then the date.

April 16, 19—

> My heart is breaking and rejoicing. My beloved daughter
> left this morning for the finishing school where her Father
> has sent her to "make a lady out of her." I rejoice because
> she has escaped this stifling and oppressive environment.

She may learn before this world has destroyed belief that she is a precious child of God: fully human, whole, beautiful, and wise. Ah! If her Father only knew ...

If he suspected that "finishing school" he so carefully chose is one of the most liberal and egalitarian institutions in the entire North!

I am confident that there my dear daughter will be freed to become ... herself, and I am equally confident that if my husband knew how carefully I had contacted old friends from my days in education who helped me to find the perfect place for Priscilla Jane; how carefully I coached the school officials so that their correspondence would have just the right note of serious concern that Priscilla become a lady; how carefully we planned the interviews to ally his suspicions that Priscilla might not receive the polishing appropriate for a Haymer lady, the polishing that I, if I had not proved myself a failure, should have given her ... But I am already so lonely and lost! The purpose for which I have lived, for which I have plotted and planned since the moment I learned that God had blessed me with a daughter, has been fulfilled. I can rest now. She has escaped. She will grow up whole. She will learn to use her mind to the fullest as I was once encouraged to do—before I was taught "my place." My daughter will be free!

Stunned, P. J. pulled out other composition books, tracing the history of her mother's systematic education of her beloved daughter, her plotting, her planning, for the escape of P. J. from the system within which she herself had remained trapped. Her mother's love oozed from every page along with her concern that P. J. learn that the black children with whom she had surreptitiously learned and played were her equals, no more, no less. Stories of her concern, of her watchfulness that P. J. not be overwhelmed by her father's heavy manner, by the family demands, by the lack of encouragement of academic performance by P. J.'s teachers.

P. J. read on voraciously, giddily, and then wearily, sometimes weeping softly, until she had drunk in the whole story, until the light of the setting sun cast only pale, golden shadows into Mother's place. P. J. closed the last book. So she had been neither abandoned nor betrayed. The mother, of whom all these years she had detested her weakness and fled, had been a ghost, a fantasy of her mind. *And now, at the time of her death, the real woman—strong and loving and wise—is at last alive for me.* So Mother had nurtured her strengths and gifts, had been proud of the rebellious daughter with the inappropriate behavior. Mother had ... loved her.

Grief welled up in P. J. as she slowly descended the stairs. "I cannot thank her now ... and I ... I never knew her," P. J. murmured in the empty hall, as if to excuse the tears streaming down her face. She paused for a final look around, started out, paused again, and then turned toward the painting of her father.

P. J. turned it back around so the steely gaze once again confronted her. With a voice of strength and authority, P. J. addressed her father's portrait. "Father, you were wrong. Your schools didn't make me a lady of me. They made a human being of me, a healed and whole person, such as my mother was, and I didn't even know it. And, Father ... my mother knew her place. It was on the cross your hatred made for her. Your jealousy and pride crucified her, demeaned her fine mind. But you were no match for her. Her goodness, her love, her wisdom triumphed, Father. I am not a lady; I am my mother's daughter. And I could ask for no more."

P. J. lifted the tilted frame high and hung it in its accustomed place. Was the painting smaller, the gaze less fierce? "I am not afraid, Father. And I see that I have the same fierce gaze as the one that once terrorized me. I didn't even know I was your daughter as well.

"Now I see that the father I hated, judged, condemned for his destructive criticism, his forgiving spirit, was alive in me! You live yet, Father. Perhaps someday I can learn to celebrate the strengths I have received from you and forgive ... forgive you? Forgive myself?"

Sadness suddenly swept over P. J., and she paused for a long moment before continuing in a whisper, "You ... you, too, were trapped, my father. Trapped in the system that said the Haymers were guardians of communal values, trapped in a system that said blacks were inferior and women were objects to be cared for and kept silent. I didn't know you either, my father. Did your anger hide your tears? Your love? Your fear that you might fail the systems?" P. J. stood silently before the painting, peering intently into the gray, unblinking eyes as if to read some message. Then she turned and crossed the hall, stepped into the soft evening air, and closed the door.

The row of blossoming trees stretched before her, and she walked briskly to the spot where her tree had been, the third from the left. *I wonder when my tree was cut down and replaced*, she mused as she drew near to the lovely, bloom-filled, straight tree that stood in its place. She reached up to steady herself against the rough trunk that still bore the faint scars where a collar had once encircled it. This beautiful tree was hers! Scarred, yes, but beautiful. The tree, even with the restrictions of the collar, had somehow been nourished and had survived. Like P. J., strangled, scarred. But not deformed ... and not rootless.

The collar I fought and fled shaped and defined me. My mother kept it loose enough so that the racial and sexual restraints that would have strangled me didn't destroy me. She provided a place large enough for me to stretch and grow. And to do this she sacrificed her own growth; she accepted the imprisonment for me. I ... I am Miz Lily's final effects.

Reluctantly, P. J. turned toward the small rented car, feeling the pressure of preparing to greet Miz Lily's last visitors at the funeral home. Time enough tomorrow to think about mother's last effects.

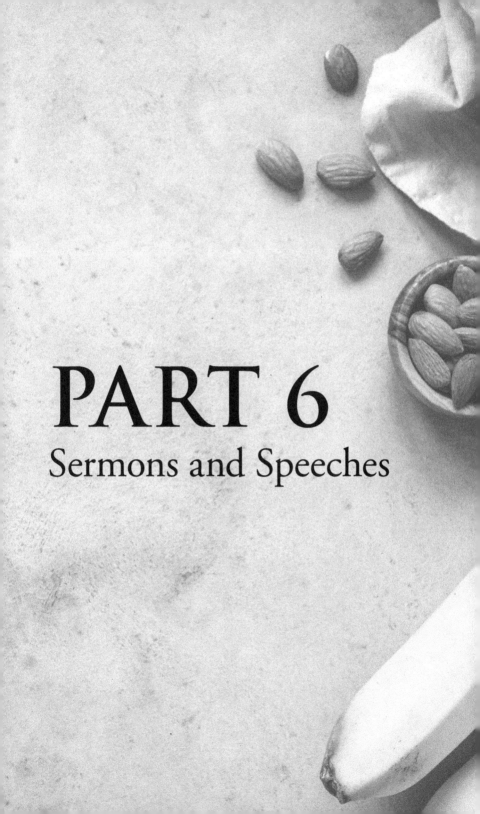

PART 6

Sermons and Speeches

68

Where the Roaring Lion Prowls

Scripture: 1 Peter 4:12–19

Edward Hicks, *The Peaceable Kingdom*, 1834.
National Gallery of Art, Washington DC.

The yellow eyes gaze out at us from dark, tropical growth. Wild beasts stare solemnly, like overmedicated patients from the undergrowth. Static, unthreatening, peaceful, the creatures startle and surprise us with the unreality of the scene. You are looking at the famous American primitive painting *The Peaceable Kingdom*. You are surprised because you know jungles are where predators prowl and death lurks. The lion and the lamb don't *really* lie down together. You know that the jungles are where the roaring lion prowls.

You know what the world is like, as did the author of 1 Peter 5:8, who warned his beloved readers to beware of a roaring lion, which growls about, looking for someone to devour. "Do not be surprised," he says, "at the fiery ordeal that is taking place among you, as though something strange were happening to you" (1 Peter 4:12 NRSV). Perhaps those readers had hoped for a peaceable kingdom where Christian brothers and sisters could live in serenity and security. A nice dream, which might have caught their wishful, hopeful minds as the *Peaceable Kingdom* catches ours.

But then, as Robert Frost says in his poem "Birches," "Truth broke in with all her matter-of-fact." The author of the Petrine epistle adds that ordeals are nothing strange for Christians; ordeals are part of the territory. And with those words in the letter sent to the churches of Asia Minor, a chilling message spread; if you are a Christian, you can expect trouble. We don't know what fiery ordeal prompted the writing of this letter. We don't know what actions by the Christians provoked the admonitions to avoid committing various crimes and to avoid making mischief. But we do know that lions—in the form of oppression or harassment or exclusion or official persecution—prowled around the community, and lions prowled, both within and without the hearts of those Christians, exiles of the dispersion in Pontus, Galatia, Cappadocia, Asia, and Bithynia. We don't know what fiery ordeal prompted the writing of this letter. We don't know what actions by the Christians provoked the admonitions to avoid committing various crimes and to avoid making mischief. But we do know that lions—in the form of oppression or harassment or exclusion or official persecution—prowled around the community, and lions prowled both within and without the hearts of those Christians, exiles of the dispersion in Pontus, Galatia, Cappadocia, Asia, and Bithynia.

And the letter comes to them, saying, "But rejoice in so far as you are sharing Christ's sufferings, so that you may also be glad and shout for joy when his glory is revealed. If you are reviled for the name of Christ, you are blessed because the spirit of glory which is the Spirit of God rests upon you" (1 Peter 4:13 NRSV). Strong words! Powerful words to those scattered house churches separated by distance and fear from Rome, from comrades, from others who could encourage and console and fight the lion with them. Rejoice! Rejoice! Though the roaring lion prowl about you, seeking those whom he may devour, rejoice, for you suffer for Christ. And are we so different, my friends, scattered as we are among the peoples of the world, attacked by discouragement and fear and loneliness and defeatism? Are we so different, surrounded as we are by systems and institutions that oppose the values of the church, the mission, and purposes of the people of God? We, too, suffer for Christ's sake. But the author of 1 Peter says suffering is inevitable. Cheap grace isn't grace at all. "Human beings are born to trouble as the sparks fly upward" (Job 5:7 NRSV). You might as well expect to encounter hostility and danger in life if you are a Christian. The dream of the peaceable kingdom is just that: a dream that is strangely wonderful to see in a painting but not part of the reality we live in.

"It's not fair! It's not right!" we may protest, as did the victim in Shirley Jackson's chilling story "The Lottery." But we know with a strangely empty feeling, a sense of helplessness of humankind, of the essential tragic nature of life, that life may not be fair and right as we believe it should be. Suffering is inevitable. Justice may just be a dream that glows in the golden eyes of otherworldly creatures frozen forever in artist's vision.

Then what is it all about? What are we doing here? To what purpose do we gather seeking the gospel? Where is the good news? In what shall we rejoice? For what shall we glorify God?

The author of 1 Peter would reply, "If you are reviled for the name of Christ, you are blessed, the spirit of glory is the Spirit of God is residing on you" (1 Peter 4:13 NRSV). Blessed? Happy? How so? "Trust," he replies. "Therefore, let those suffering in accordance with God's will entrust themselves to a faithful Creator, while continuing to do good" (1 Peter 4:19 NRSV). In those quiet words is more peace and assurance than all those golden eyes of the peaceable kingdom, more joy and hope than all the world can offer. Trust the Creator evokes in us the echo of a truth, made in the divine image of the creator ... a little lower than the angels ... hope. Will not he who fashioned us, wonderfully and fearfully made, save us from the lions that prowl within and without?

Beloved, don't be surprised. You are sent out as sheep among wolves, where the roaring lion prowls, to live in the world, to wrestle with the dark beasts of your own heart. Suffering is inevitable.

But there still comes that recurring dream, that strange vision of the quiet beasts, dreamy eyed and still. Shivers of hope echo softly, "But rejoice in so far as you are sharing in Christ's sufferings so that you may also be glad and shout for joy when his glory is revealed" (1 Peter 4:13 NRSV).

The songwriter Dr. Bryson E. Bell asks, "Must Jesus bear the cross alone and all the world go free? No, there's a cross for everyone, and there's a cross for me." We are called by Christ's name and by Christ to take up a cross, to walk in the inevitable path of suffering for him. And that is glory. Such glory makes us able to endure the beasts—discouragement, loneliness, uncertainty, weariness, doubt—that prowl in our hearts. Such glory enables us to speak out against the prowling beasts of this world, who say that in military stockpiles lies a peaceable kingdom, who say that in political intervention by the strong—us—lies the salvation of the developing nations.

We, like the Christians to whom the letter 1 Peter was addressed, are the household of God scattered throughout the lands, distrusted for our convictions and lifestyle, provoking animosity and suspicion when we suggest that making war may not be making peace. We are reproached because we bear the name of the Prince of Peace, reproached because we dream of a peaceable kingdom, where all persons may be full citizens. And we witness to our dream out there, where the roaring lion prowls. For us, as for those other Christians in Asia Minor, the author of I Peter says, God is faithful, be thou faithful, be strong; Hang in and hang together. Accept suffering but don't seek it out. And above all, rejoice and give glory to the One whose name you bare.

Let it be so. Amen.

69

He Died Alone

Scripture: John 18–19 (selected verses)

When I was about twenty-five years old, someone asked me, "What is your greatest fear?"

"I don't know," I answered. I said that in part because I really hadn't asked myself that question before. I gave the answer, "I don't know," in part because I wasn't sure that I wanted to tell anyone the answer, even if I did know.

I tried to ignore the question, but it kept probing my mind, like one's tongue keeps probing at the sharp corner left after he or she chips a tooth.

Finally, I realized that my greatest fear was that I would die and that no one would find my body for several days. The greatest fear wasn't dying alone. The greatest fear wasn't having my body found until after many days. The real fear was that I would be so alone that I wouldn't have anyone close enough to even notice I had died.

My greatest fear is of having no relationships, no person with whom I share a friendship sufficiently close that he or she would notice whether my routine was varied by death. My fear is of being completely alone. It is a fear, I have learned, that is shared by many. A fellow was telling me recently that his wife died a little over a year ago and that he had a terrible year. He said he knew it would be tough because they had been very close and had done everything together. But he had had no idea how tough it would be. He had been terrified of being alone, he said. After the interment service, while people were still at the cemetery, he had been seized by terror and had gone up to people and pleaded, "Now remember, I'm still around. Don't forget that I'm still here." I understand his terror of being alone. I remember several years ago being awakened by the telephone in the middle of the night. As I fumbled, dazed by sleep, for the phone, I saw that it was three thirty in the morning. "Mary," my father's weary voice whispered. "She's gone. She died in my arms a few minutes ago." Even beyond the weariness and the grief in his voice, I could hear relief. He was relieved that his beloved wife hadn't had to die alone.

Truly fear of loneliness seems to be pervasive among us humans. That is why it seems so poignantly sad that Jesus died alone. He was deserted, betrayed, rejected, mocked. He was abandoned by all but a few women—his mother among them; a disciple, who loved him enough to watch the horror of the crucifixion; and a nameless person, who brought him something to wet his dry mouth.

He was ignored by the soldiers, who were more interested in seeing who would get his tunic than in being with him in his final moments. He was just a job to them and a chance to pick up a few items to sell. They cared nothing for the agony of his final moments. Jesus died alone, and, most terrible of all, it seemed God abandoned him too.

We humans often deserve our aloneness. The disciples ended up alone in part because they were weak. Judas betrayed because he thought he knew best and wanted to control the outcome of events. Peter became afraid of the cost of friendship and betrayed him alone by the servants' fire. Others, afraid and confused, scattered and hid out alone in their terror. Many disappeared because they hadn't paid enough attention to what Jesus had been teaching them to trust that all would be well. Like the disciples, we may be alone because of our own misguided choices.

- We drive others away because we are always right.
- We fear to risk commitment to intimacy or friendship because the demands may be too great; we fear losing our power, our voice, ourselves to another.
- We hide out—*cocoon* is the new in word for it—renting videos, watching TV, avoiding involvement with the real world and real relationships we cannot turn on and off at will.
- We fear to trust—fearing we have too much to lose, then out of fear lose everything that's important—family, friends, and colleagues.
- We forget the hope-filled promises of Christ.

Or we may be alone because of the sins of others.

- Others may be rigidly sure they are always right and unwilling to respect us if we disagree.
- Others may be unable to trust and spurn our attempt at friendship.
- Others may hide out, unwilling to commit the great gifts of time and caring that make enduring relationships possible.
- Others may be unwilling to forgive our honest mistakes.

Whether we deserve our aloneness or not, we know Jesus didn't deserve to be alone. He became alone by choice through no sin or weakness of his own.

- He chose the intense, complete aloneness of the humiliating trial and death of a criminal.
- He chose to take our sin on himself.
- He chose, even and most awfully, separation from God, total aloneness, for us to enter into death is to be separated from God, who is life. To become sin for us is to choose to become separated from God, who is goodness and righteousness and truth.

Those were the choices Jesus made for you and me so we would never be totally alone. Whatever the reasons, they—the disciples and Jesus—were all alone on that first Good Friday, God's Friday. Each disciple was alone in his particular terror, his particular grief, in the loss of his particular hopes or dreams. The ache, the grief, the loneness must have been almost unendurable. Having been with Emmanuel—God with us—for so long, how might they have endured their total aloneness? They knew what promises Jesus had left with them.

- "I have called you friends" (John 15:15 NRSV).
- "I will not leave you desolate. I will come to you. Yet a little while, and the world will see me no more, but you will see me; because I live, you will live also" (John 14:18–19 NRSV).

These promises were so soon forgotten in their loneliness and desolation. The deepest fear of humanity had become reality in them, for they didn't know the promises were yet to be fulfilled. No wonder they ran.

- They thought they stood behind the right of God, the might of God.
- They thought they'd stood with the power of God in the hour of God.
- They stood composed, naked, totally vulnerable, and left, believing Jesus was, after all, only a minor political agitator.
- Alone they shivered; alone they trembled.
- And then he was dead. Dead! Their hopes were shattered, their dreams also dead.
- The one who had given them a vision of God's new reign was dead, and they were alone.
- Nobody remembered or knew there was to be a resurrection.

And what of Jesus? Where was he? In death. In death's cold bonds by choice. He had been completely in tune with the voice, the call, the will of God, not alone, having chosen death, so that our deepest fears need never become reality. What has this to do with us? What is the good news? What is the word of hope in this awe-filled story?

Jesus has taught us how to live in the full range of human existence.

- He showed us that only in risk is there hope of release from our aloneness. In every friendship there is potential for betrayal. But only where there is love and a commitment can a relationship, which a cure for our loneliness, endure.
- Jesus shows us that love is greater than hate, that we may choose how we respond to the rejection and betrayal of others, that we must choose the response of love and forgiveness if we are to live fully.
- We may choose to respond to life and to those whom we encounter with anger, resentment, or revenge, but to do so is to enter a tomb of our own constructing, to build the walls up stone by stone until they meet across our heads and become a tomb in which we are alone.

- Jesus shows us the kind of friend he is—one who will never reject or forsake us, no matter how little able to be a faithful friend we are. It was as Judas came to betray him that Jesus called him "friend."
- Jesus shows us the effects of our prejudices. When we reject any people who are different and judge them as unacceptable, when we place them outside the gates, we discover to our horror and shock that Jesus is with them, that Jesus, who was crucified outside the wall of the city, is outside the gate with the least and the lost. And *we* are left alone. The authorities who wouldn't listen to the truth of the prophet from Nazareth found themselves alone in the city ... with God outside the gate.
- And Jesus shows us that even when we through anger distrust, or when fear builds up a wall around us and we wall ourselves off from human relationships, we discover we aren't alone. Jesus is with us in the tombs we make. Jesus, who suffered the tomb after his crucifixion, comes to us in our own tombs and gently, lovingly befriends us. And he lovingly invites us forth into relationships with him. He invites us to risk relationships with other in his name.

On that Good Friday long ago, there was darkness over the earth. Was there also darkness inside those who had known and loved and followed Jesus? Was it as if the light had gone out inside them? He died and was buried ... and with him died their hopes. "But we had hoped, but we had hoped that He" (Luke 24:21 NRSV); they moaned as they stumbled toward Emmaus in their grief. He was dead, and they were alone, and hope seemed dead as well.

If we are to retain any thought of Good Friday through this coming year, let it be these images:

- Jesus alone on the cross
- His followers, family, friends alone

Let us remember these images so that when we are struggling, the deep loneliness of fear or loss or rejection, we may remember. Out of that terrible aloneness, which all of us as humans endure, whether it be loss of a spouse, betrayal of a colleague, desertion by a friend, loss of dreams, or estrangement from family, may come our cry. "Jesus, my friend. Come to me! Save me from my aloneness in sin!"

Let these images give you hope so you may feel the comforting presence of the one who doesn't change your circumstances but walks with you and strengthens you so you may endure all.

He died alone … so we may never be alone again.

Thanks be to God. Amen.*

---

* Mary was the district superintendent of the Decatur District in the Central Illinois Conference when she preached this sermon at the Elwin United Methodist Church on Good Friday, April 9, 1993.

70

Beyond the Angels

Scripture: John 20:1–18

On this glorious Easter morning, it may be difficult for us to imagine what it was like on that first Easter at sunrise.

It must have been a morning that began with grief so deep that those who had loved and followed Jesus doubted the sun would rise. The horrible image of their beloved Jesus crucified, dead, and buried must have been burned into their minds and hearts, seared into their very souls. Then the morning brought new shock and surprise.

Coming to the tomb early, the women found the stone rolled away and questions, uncertainty, fear … and new grief began. Mary summoned Simon Peter and John to see that the stone had been rolled away.

They ran in a strange, sad footrace to see an empty tomb. And John, it says, believed. What he believed and what he understood and what new questions came simmering into the minds of both, we don't know. But Simon Peter and John went away to their own homes, perhaps to think. They didn't see the angels.

Mary was alone in her own intense grief and now concern about what might have been done with the body of Jesus.

Stunned already, she must have been totally unhinged by the sight of … angels! One was at the head, and one was at the foot of the place where Jesus's body had lain. Yet Mary in her pain was ministered to by angels, the messengers from God.

In such desperate grief that she couldn't think, couldn't remember, Mary was asked a question. "Woman, why are you weeping?" the angel at the head asked (John 20:13 NRSV). The being shimmered with light, who had carefully rolled up the piece of cloth that had covered Jesus's head, and he called out to her gently, "Women, why are you weeping?" (John 20:13 NRSV).

It was a question to shock the heart already broken and in despair. But it was also a question that began ... very ... slowly ... to quicken the mind stunned by grief ... to tap at it just so until ... slowly ... beyond the borders of memory ... a phrase ... what was it ... what was it he said? "I will ... on the third day, I will on the third day I will rise again. Rise again! Rise again!"

New confusion, new questions within the already-reeling mind of Mary. Did he? Is that where? Could it be? Did he literally mean that he? Then the angel at the feet, with a grand and sweeping embracing, announcing gesture, flung out his arms and arrested her attention. Mary's broken heart quickened as she turned ...

With eyes blurred and red with weeping, accustomed to the dim light of the tomb, Mary turned into the glorious light of the new day and clearly saw a figure. From the person's lips she heard again the question "Woman, why are you weeping?" (John 20:15 NRSV). Deep in her grief, Mary still heard only with her head and responded to him as to a gardener, a stranger, someone who might know where the body had been taken. Then Jesus spoke her name, and her heart responded at last with recognition, with joy. "*Rabbouni!*" (which means "Teacher") (John 20:16 NRSV). And in a natural response of worship and love, she moved to embrace him. Jesus cautioned her to stop holding onto him and sent her to tell his brothers and sisters—those who had lived and followed him—to tell them he would ascend to God. The angels ministered to Mary so she could more easily endure the shock of seeing Jesus alive again. They prepared her, heart and mind, just a little so she might not be overcome by seeing her Lord alive.

But why angels? Surely there was no need on this day, this day that was to become most joyful, for angels. Wouldn't it have been sufficient for Jesus to appear to announce and show that he was risen from the grave? Why angels?

It helps me to imagine an answer to that question when I think about what had happened since Jesus's body lay there, wrapped—along with some hundred pounds of spices—in the long linen shroud, the head covered by a separate cloth. Dead.

We don't know what happened after that on Shabbat, Sabbath, Holy Day, or Saturday, depending on your calendar. One ancient tradition calls that time "the harrowing hell." This tradition says Christ descended into Hades between the time of his crucifixion and resurrection to bring salvation to all those of faith who had died before his coming. He is pictured leading Adam by one hand and Eve by another, with Abraham and Sarah, Isaac and Rebekah, Jacob, and a great cloud of the early faithful ones out of the place of the dead.

Another ancient tradition calls it "laughing Saturday," when Christ and all the angels looked Satan in the face and laughed triumphantly until the courts of heaven and the caverns of Hades rang and echoed and shook with cosmic laughter.

I don't know what happened during that time.

I do know that Jesus, having cried out, "My God, My God! Why have you forsaken me?" (Mark 33:34 NRSV), died. And he was taken down from the cross and buried, alone. And he lay. Abandoned. Forsaken. In death, he who had been so fully alive, who had been so close to God, became separated from God, who is life. In taking our sins upon himself, in becoming sin for us, he became separated from God, who is holy and righteous. Jesus was alone. And God, from whom Jesus was then separated in death, must have wept, along with those who had followed Jesus to Jerusalem. I like to think God didn't want Jesus to be alone and to feel forsaken any longer than was absolutely necessary. I like to think that is why those angels were there: waiting for Jesus to be resurrected from the dead. I believe the angels had sat there, one at his feet and one at his head, while his body lay on the cold slab. And as that body awakened to life ... awakened to *life*, when he made that shocking and amazing journey back, they were there so he who had cried out on the cross, "My God! My God! Why have you forsaken me?" (Mark 33:34 NRSV), would know instantly when he returned to consciousness, that he was forsaken no more.

Whatever happened as his empty shell was refilled with the spirit of life, with breath, with consciousness? They sat with him. At last he stirred, and they were there—comforting him, steadying him.

As a mother and father minister to their child who has cried out in a bad dream and rouses from sleep, the angels were there, ministering to him. Love, strength, the presence surrounded him through the messengers of God. He was surrounded and supported by the love of the one beyond the angels.

Perhaps Jesus sat a few moments on the cold slab where his body had lain as blood and joy thundered in his ears. Then he stood with a shout of joy. "O death where is thy sting? O grave where is thy victory?" (1 Corinthians 15:55 KJV).

Why angels? Jesus wouldn't have asked that question. When they came to arrest him in the garden and one of his followers drew his sword and cut off an ear of one who had come to seize Jesus, Jesus told his friend to put away his sword. Jesus reminded him that he could call out legions of angels, who would come rescue him. Why not angels? "For He will command His angels concerning you to guard you in all your ways," the scriptures tell us (Psalm 91:11 NRSV).

Angels are a popular topic now. Perhaps we are hungry for a sense that God still speaks to us in our human existence. A series of books about angels have been best sellers in the past few years. One of my friends, who has struggled with cancer and the painful, debilitating treatments it necessitated, has found much comfort in the angel books. But, she says, it has been the real angels—the flesh and blood friends— who have given her strength and encouragement and God's visible love through it all.

Look then beyond the angels and see an empty tomb. And know that Jesus was there before you and that you no longer need fear death. Bill Henson, pastor of one of our larger churches in Texas, told of a time when his daughter Cathy's cat died, and they went at once to let her pick out a new pet. She chose a puppy. Trying to be a good father, Bill built a doghouse for the puppy. He was unaccustomed to building anything. He said the doghouse was so large that it scared the little Peekapoo. He wouldn't go near it. Bill put his food in there, and he would go hungry; he would put his water in there, and he would go thirsty. In exasperation, Bill shoved him in and held his hands over the door, but the minute he moved, the dog ran out, unbelievably frightened. Bill finally gave up and went into the house, leaving his daughter to cry about her puppy's refusal to go into the doghouse.

After a time, Cathy got down on her hands and knees, and crawled into the doghouse. When she did, something really wonderful happened. That little puppy just trotted right in beside her and stretched out on the doghouse floor. Soon he was taking a nap. Suddenly, all the shadows stood still for him, and all the dread was taken out of the darkness, because one whom he loved and trusted had gone before him into the dark and frightened place.

Ah, yes! When we look beyond the angels into the tomb, we see that Jesus preceded us into death. And because he went before us, death has lost its sting for us too. He preceded us into that dark and frightening place, and the shadows stand still. The dread of the darkness is seen in a different light. We see beyond that darkness to the light of eternal life, to a savior who walked the road to death before us to a God whose loving arms reach through the darkness to embrace us.

Look beyond the angels and see the empty tomb. And know that Jesus was there before you and that you need have no fear.

Stand then in the darkness of the tomb and look beyond the angels. See then a world hurting, despairing. See a world that desperately needs to hear the brush of angels' wings, the glorious voice of angel choirs raised in alleluias. See beyond the angels to a world that urgently needs to hear, "He is not here; he is risen, just as he said." (Matthew 28:6 NIV).

"Do not hold onto me" (John 20:17 NRSV), Jesus commanded Mary. Stop holding onto me and go and tell. You go, too. Go and tell that he is alive. That he goes before us. That he tells us brother, sister, friend. That he walks with us in our darkest hours. Help others to see beyond the strangeness and wonder of the angel messengers to an even greater wonder: a loving God who doesn't forsake but calls each of us, each of them, God's beloved child. Go and tell how our darkest despair is made light in the glory of Easter.

Go and become flesh-and-blood angels who bring comfort and hope to those in pain. Go to make God's love visible for those who don't know they are loved.

Beyond the angels is life, life abundant, radiant life in Christ. Go and tell. And may the risen Christ be with you on your journey.

71

The Idolatry of Place

Scripture: Hebrews 11:1–3; 8–10; 14–16

How precious is the place where we first came to faith! Forever after we have memories, which come forth when we come to worship, hear the hymns, pray, or seek God. We remember and are glad for the place that was our first spiritual home.

I once took a friend on a trip to see the places of my childhood. The house, barn, crib, and orchard were gone. Only the cemetery and the bell, now placed in a four-foot-high tower with a plaque, remained.

The town church, my grandmother's church, the place where I had poured out my questions, where I had sat on the steps and talked to and about God, the place where I had accepted Jesus Christ as *my* personal savior was already gone—burned down in a fire. I had known that, had heard of its destruction, but was still unprepared for the grief I felt when I saw the now-empty lot. I remembered the saints who had worshipped there. I went out to the new church at the edge of town and wondered how the aging saints who had walked to the old, redbrick church in their neighborhood got to the new one on the edge of town.

I took a while during and after the trip to reflect on my feelings and thoughts about those places. The words of God from the Letter to the Hebrews came to me. I have called you to step out, like Abram and Sarai, on faith. Do not yearn for a place on this earth; yearn for the eternal place I am preparing for you. Do not hold back in fear but step out on faith, for I am with you.

I learned then of my idolatry—my idolatry of place. I had made an idol of a place, wanting it to be forever available so I might worship there. It was all right for me to grieve its passing, to love the place as Bethel, God's house, where I met God, but it wasn't all right to lift it up as an idol, for God wasn't there alone. God was before me, calling me to go forth into whatever future God had for me.

Set out on faith, as did Abram and Sarai, to follow me on faith.

To cling to space—even sacred space—is idolatrous. To have another god before Yahweh, Jehovah, is idolatrous. Our God is a living God, who constantly calls us forward on faith.

- To go forward to new places and be faithful
- To go out to proclaim God's love to us in Jesus
- To make disciples

Since there is nothing in scripture about retirement, we are called to this work for God all our lives … all our lives.

For the individual to make an idol is sin—death. So when we cling to life instead of eternal life with God, we fall short of God's plan for us and risk the loss of our immortal souls and a home in the city God prepares for us eternally.

For a congregation to make an idol is also death. We risk death when we make an idol of our church. When we ask a congregation to cling to our family chapel and demand that it remain open for us alone and don't work for the kingdom of God, we commit idolatry. When the missionaries aren't supported, when the gospel isn't proclaimed through our gifts, we cling to what is here rather than yearn for that perfect city made for us by God. And we risk death.

We don't choose our mission. We cannot say, "Well, we will do this without regard for God's will." Instead we must ask, "What does God want us to do?" God gives us a mission and invites us—yes, commands us—to fulfill it. Faithfulness depends on our responding to God's mission. A faithful response is going out on faith, not knowing where the strength or money will come from for our conference claims, for our service to the community.

Our human tendency is to respond to God's call with fear, not faith. We cling to what we can see rather than rest on faith that God will go with us into the unknown, until at last we see that perfect city, which God has prepared. And when we live by fear, oh, what glory we miss! It is a joyful thing; it is a glorious thing to live by faith and to prove God's presence and power. To fulfill God's purpose in the world through Jesus Christ is the only way we find peace.

When Peter walked on the water, he started out on faith, looking at Jesus, believing in the power of the Lord. Then fear came when he saw the height of the waves, and he began to sink. When we live by faith, we walk on. When we live by fear, we sink. This is true of the individual. This is true of the church.

Christ calls today. He calls you and you and you and me. Will we dare to respond in faith? Speak, Lord, bid me walk on the water. Hold me up. Instruct me in what you would have me do.

Will we respond in fear? We can't do that. We are too old; there are too few of us. The waves are too high.

Will God be ashamed to be called our God? Do we believe and yearn and long for the city whose builder and architect is God? Or do we make an idol of a place, this place, and turn from the one who offers eternal life?

When Christ calls us today, what will our answer be?*

---

* Mary preached this sermon at the Oconee/Ohlman United Methodist Churches on September 24, 1995.

72

Healed for Wholeness

Scriptures: Psalm 30:2–5; Luke 8:24b–46 and 49–56

She lived on the fringes of society. For twelve years she had been there, shut out from all activities, isolated, ashamed. Sometimes she wondered whether she had committed some terrible sin. She heard it whispered of her. She was unclean, and people hurried by her if she chanced to be visible, passing as far away from her as possible, not speaking, averting their eyes. Sometimes she felt invisible. Always she felt ashamed. There were times when were it not for the continuous pain and bleeding, she might have wondered whether she really did exist.

Then she began to hear stories about a teacher, one who had unusual power to heal. Even from her isolated station on the fringe, she heard the stories. And she began to imagine a daring plan. At first it was more daydream than plan, a wish that kept her going when she didn't think she could stand being alone any longer.

Then the dream became an audacious hope, a scheme to approach the healer. Did she dare? Did she dare to venture out into public, to push into a crowd and risk further condemnation, possibly even death at the hands of those who would condemn her for violating the code they lived by? *What have I to lose?* she argued with herself when her courage almost failed her. *I am as if dead to everyone now. What is death to me who lives as one dead to my community? I will dare to go to where he is teaching. Perhaps if I but reach out from the fringes of society to touch the fringe of his clothes, I shall be healed.*

You know the rest of the story. She *was* healed. But that's not *all* the story. Then … then she was made whole as she came into relationship, into community. She came into wholeness, which is only possible when one is more than an I. Her wholeness came from the name, the title, the position that was bestowed on her. How did it happen? It happened in the part of the story we didn't read. Listen! "Who touched me?" Jesus asked. When all denied it, Peter said, "Master the crowds surround you and press in on you" (Luke 8:45-46 NRSV). But Jesus said, "Someone touched me, for I noticed that power had gone out of me" (Luke 8:45-46 NRSV). When the woman saw that she couldn't remain hidden, she came trembling and falling down before him; she declared in the presence of all the people why she had touched him and that she had immediately been healed. He said to her, "Daughter, your faith has made you well, go in peace" (Luke 8:48 NRSV).

"Daughter." With that title, she who had been shunned, pushed aside to the fringes of life, had been returned to community. She became part once more of the people of God. People of her community who heard that word *daughter* would perhaps hear the whole phrase, "Daughter of Abraham." We hear "Daughter of God," and in that hearing we also hear "sister of Christ" and "My sister."

She had been healed, freed of disease. Then she was made whole. In the ancient tradition out of which our present faith has grown understood well, there is more to wellness than the absence of disease. From the same root come both the word *salvation* and the word *healed*. They understood that our whole selves—minds, bodies, and spirits—must be brought into balance and healthy relationship with self, others, and God before we are truly whole. "Daughter," Jesus said to the woman. And she who had been healed in body was again recognized as one in relationship with God and community. In that affectionate name she was recognized as part of Israel, part of the family.

It saddens me that we don't see her living out her life so she could be a model to us today of a whole woman, a healed woman living a life of joyful service in response to God's love. I would like to see how she helped her community become healed as well from its disease.

We can imagine and hope that the hurt she had endured would make her sensitive to the plight of others who lived on the fringes of society, those who were lonely, shamed, forgotten, powerless, invisible.

Instead of seeing her healer, we are given a picture of the twelve disciples. They saw him heal the woman from her illness of twelve years. Some of them—Peter, James, and John—saw him heal another daughter, a child of twelve, around whom the mourners had already gathered. And having seen him perform these and many other acts of healing, they were given power to heal and sent out with instruction for doing so. They themselves had been gathered up and healed of their isolation, their smallness of faith and life, their doubts, their alienation from God and been brought into a community of healed persons and become whole. Out of their wholeness they are given power to go out and heal.

That seems to be the model Christ has given us and which we see at numerous points in scripture; Christ is present. People come to him and reach out. And he responds, discovering us as we are: poor, wretched, blind, lonely, afraid, hurting, doubting, angry, weary, frustrated, distrusting, wounded, bruised—in all the battered states in which we are left when life flings us aside. And even in the reaching out, our healing begins. Then in response, we are healed for wholeness. We are called "Daughter," "My Beloved Child," "My Son," "Friend." And in that naming, we are made whole as we enter into relationship and learn to care for others.

We are no longer alone. Our fear is diminished. We gain new perspectives. What was once our little story—the story of one person alone in the universe—is woven together into the story of God, a beautiful and forever story. We are part of something bigger than ourselves. We can't see it all, but we have hope. We can't understand it all. But we know we are not alone. We know we are at one with mystery. And we know that beyond what we can see—the temporary, the finite, the mortal—we are connected to the infinite and the immortal.

As my kids say, "Pretty awesome!"

"Pretty awesome!"

It keeps happening over and over, this healing of persons as the love of God is poured out to us in the name of Jesus Christ. And when we are healed, we become whole and part of a whole that is greater than ourselves, become concerned for others.

United Methodist Women are a beautiful example of this. We know the flow of being healed for wholeness. We come to know in some intimate way of God's love for us. Knowing ourselves to be loved of God, we become part of a group that is seeking healing for others—healing of injustice, healing of hunger, poverty, illiteracy, oppression, disease. Having received the healing touch, we become whole and reach to offer healing and hope to a wounded world.

It would be a great mistake for us to think that the story of the woman suffering with an infirmity for twelve years was only a story of someone long ago. She lives today. She lives among us by the dozens, hundreds, thousands. She lives on the fringes of our lives. Must she wait until driven to total despair to be healed? Could we not notice those who dwell on the fringes of our lives and reach out and call them "Daughter" or "Friend?"

United Methodist Women can do that. They do that. United Methodist Women at their very best do reach out.

But before we congratulate ourselves too much, we must ask, Who are we, by social prejudice, excluding from our circles, overlooking, shoving to the fringes? Is it the working woman? Are they single parents who have no childcare they can trust? Are they women of color? Are they divorced women?

We do so much good for so many as United Methodist Women. Nevertheless, I believe we are continually challenged by the question. Are there women who stand on the fringes because we aren't reaching out to them? The church and all its ministries are entrusted to us by our Lord. We are stewards to carry on the work as it would please him. If he visited your circle, your Sunday school class, your Bible study, any of the groups that are part of your life, would he go away, sadly shaking the dust from his sandals because the message hadn't been heard? I pray not. I pray that you and the groups of which you are part—especially your circles—are healthy ones, healed and whole and seeking to bring healing and good news of God's love to others. Before you say, "It is just not in me to do that. I can't talk to strangers. I'm not comfortable," remember they aren't strangers. They are sisters. God is parent of us all.

Maybe you think it isn't your gift to reach out. But there are plenty of ways you might bring healing. People can be heard into wholeness. Regular telephone calls to those who are lonely will bring healing to them. They wouldn't call you. They don't want to bother you. They don't want to be a burden. But oh, how they would love to hear a voice, a voice that asks them how they are and then listens—really listens—before they hang up or go away. How many skins are waiting for a touch, a pat on the shoulder or hand? In this touch-shy world, many are aching to be touched. The touch that heals comes in many ways to heal in Christ's name.

Long ago one came and drew others to himself and to God. They were healed and made whole. And this keeps happening. You and I or another individual has a hurt or sees a wrong or feels a need. We reach out and find the hand of Christ reaching for us.

Oh, it may not look like the hand of Christ. It may seem to be the hand of a neighbor or friend; it may be someone in your circle or your Sunday school class or the next person in the check-out lane who says, "I know what you mean. Go ahead and talk about it. I'm listening." "I'm sorry you're hurting. How can I help?" "I've seen it too. What can we do about it?" And you are not alone; you are healed, and you find yourself propelled beyond the threshold of your own life to try to make a difference for someone else. You go as empty-handed servants. Your bread for the journey is your faith in Christ, your time, and your talents.

The manner of our going is clearly described. We are invited to step out on faith, to go and be grateful for what hospitality we find and be thankful when our message is received. We are invited, empowered, and sent to go, share the good news, and heal. And when we feel the power has gone out of us, we find encouragement, strength, and new hope in the community we have made together called United Methodist Women and the United Methodist Church. We read the inspirational or challenging study book, we join a study group, we share in a project, sending school supplies to children across town or across the world. We're United Methodist women and men and boys and girls, grateful for what Christ has done and is doing in our lives.

And having been healed and made whole through God's love to us in Christ, what good news we have to share! Thanks be to God! Amen.[*]

---

[*] Mary preached this sermon for United Methodist Women's Sunday, September 18, 1996, at Grace United Methodist Church in Decatur, Illinois.

73

The Stars Do Not Require It

The prophet Micah wrote, "He has told you, O Mortal, what is good" (Micah 6:8 NRSV). We believe the most perfect demonstration of what is good was shown to us in the life of Jesus Christ, in whose life we see the life of salvation—wholeness, completeness, oneness with God and others, shalom.

In the phrasing of the prophet, we are told, "The Lord requires" of us a good life. If we rephrase in the words of 1 John, we might say, "Love requires." Love requires justice, kindness, humility. We call that "self-giving love," love that cares first about other persons, the other person's well-being. This kind of love will sacrifice so the beloved becomes fully the person God designed the loved one to be.

First John says, "Beloved, since God loved us, we also ought to love one another" (1 John 4:11 NRSV). Yet we know that in very truth it's not out of a sense of duty—not out of "should," "ought," or "required"—that such a loving response to God or another person comes. In truth, we know we are invited, inspired, enabled so to love because, having experienced being loved, we are freed to love in return.

God doesn't require any more than the stars require. But if we are to live in a relationship with God, we shall be kind. We still seek justice. We shall be merciful. Annie Dillard explains,

> God does not demand that we give up our personal
> dignity, that we throw in our lot with random people,
> that we lose ourselves and turn from all that is not him.
> God needs nothing, asks nothing, like the stars. It is life
> with God that demands these things.

Experience has taught the race that if knowledge of God is the end, then these habits of life are not the means but the condition in which the means operates. You do not have to do these things; not at all. You do not have to do these things—unless you want to know God. They work on you, not on God.

You do not have to sit outside in the dark. If, however, you want to look at the stars, you will find that darkness is necessary. But the stars neither demand nor require it.[4]

The stars don't require it; but if you would see the stars, you must sit outside in the dark. God doesn't require, but if you would know God, you must live in love as God gives you grace to love—living justly with others, seeking justice for others, being kind and concerned, and caring for others in your household, community, and world, relating with humility, rather than arrogance, with others and with God.

Marriage doesn't require. Love requires. If you would live in love and God's love would live and grow in you, if you would live in a relationship that grows from this moment ever richer and fuller and beautiful, you will love the costly love that puts God and your beloved and even others before self-interests.

But marriage doesn't require. Caesar requires only that you pay a fee and procure a license to become wed. And so, you, Bruce and Jane, come here to be married, having paid the fee to Caesar. And today people will look at you and say, "Aren't they cute. See how they love one another. Look how in love they are." They will speak with a wistful hope that what they see in you may be a love that grows and spreads to bless them and the world. But marriage doesn't require that you let love grow into the fine thing of integrity that touches all your lives and all your relationships with justice and kindness and mercy. Marriage doesn't require this beyond or even between yourselves.

Marriage permits love to flatten out into a stale thing that comes of love's turning in upon itself, of the narrowing of one's horizon to—just so—the threshold of one's own house and the border of one's self interest. And the light will begin to go out in your eyes. And that which we all most fear will come to pass: "Oh, dear God, we have nothing to say to one another for the rest of our lives!" Even so the stars will still shine in the firmament, for the stars don't require any more than marriage requires. But what a fine hope will have been lost that you might know shalom, that entwining of lives that is energized by concerns beyond themselves by interrelatedness with all creation as a conscious and joyful choice.

Without this breadth of vision and concern, someday, ages and ages hence, your minds will be befuddled by too many dead dreams; you will still be toddling along together, and people will still be saying, "Aren't they cute? See how they love each other? Look how in love they are?" But the note of wistful hope will be gone from the voices, having been replaced with an edge of bitterness because of the mistaken belief that love is wasted on the old. And because even though the stars didn't require and the marriage didn't require, the world had hoped that your love would be more than a cool draught sipped by two passersby in the wilderness of life.

The world hopes your love will be as a swelling spring that refreshes many weary pilgrims who thirst for peace and justice and mercy.

May you dare that costly love, which neither the stars nor God, nor the world, nor marriage, nor any other creature may require of you, but that which freely given will bind you even more closely together, ever closer to God, and ever more in shalom, a peaceful interrelatedness with all creation.

May the God who loves you with an everlasting love empower you so to love. Let it be so.*

---

* Mary preached this as a wedding homily on June 3, 1989, at Macomb Wesley United Methodist Church.

74

Cabinet Address

Bishop Lawson, members of the final session of the Central Illinois Annual Conference, visitors, and friends, it is my honor and privilege, as the chair of the cabinet, to give you the cabinet address. You may want to take this down: 501 East Capital, Suite 212, Springfield, Illinois 62701. In addition to our address, I'd like to give you a glimpse of the particular perspective one has from that address.

But let me say that it is a joy to recognize the historic nature of this moment as well as the historic nature of this entire annual conference session. As the second woman to be a member of the cabinet and the first to serve as chair of the cabinet of the Central Illinois Conference, I celebrate with you the progress our church has made in affirming the gifts of all God's people in ministry.

Recently, the United Methodist Church observed the fortieth anniversary of the receiving of full clergy rights to women by the United Methodist Church (you may have noticed the yellow roses on our name tags as a commemoration of that anniversary). A friend called to tell me about that anniversary. The next evening, the chairperson of the pastor/parish relations committee of Oakley United Methodist Church in the Decatur District handed me a copy of their church history. Included in the history of that church, which had been an Evangelical United Brethren congregation before 1968, were the names of two women: Pastors Kalie Burke, who served from 1934–1936 (twenty years before the first women's clergy rights were recognized by the Methodist Church); and Elizabeth Thompson, who began preaching in 1906 and served Oakley in 1921. They were just two of the pioneers who have paved the way for us. And we give thanks for them and other women trailblazers as we recognize the new milestones our cabinet passed and recognize that we are blessed this year with the appointment of Cynthia A. Jones to join us at the table, making this the first year we've had two women on the cabinet.

We are all here today because of such pioneers as Kalie Burke, Elizabeth Thompson, and others, who kept the faith and the churches alive in Central Illinois. We can catch a glimpse of God's vision for our future and can celebrate because we stand on the shoulders of such giants. The faithful cloud of witnesses, our ancestors in the faith who dared to move toward their future, which is now our present, offer us inspiration as we look forward in that future God has already prepared for us and a new annual conference.

Among the cloud of witnesses who served our annual conference as district superintendents, I'd like to invite anyone who has been a district superintendent in the Central Illinois Annual Conference or the denominations that preceded it to stand and be recognized by this body for the service you have given to this annual conference. It's good to see Don Jones, Paul Unger, Miley Palmer, Frank Nessler out there. It gives us reassurance that there is life after cabinet.

We acknowledge your contributions to God's mission to the world through Jesus Christ. We also acknowledge the sacrifices made by all of Christ's servants, women and men, clergy and lay, who have gone before us. The seeds they have planted in the rich soil of Central Illinois have borne an abundant harvest we are called to reap. Yet, even as we celebrate, we acknowledge that we aren't there yet. This isn't heaven. I occasionally have a pastor parish relations committee say, "Send us a woman pastor. The church across town has one, and they are doing really well." Or when I recently took a clergywoman to a church to be introduced as their new pastor, the committee members said, "Welcome! We've had a woman pastor, and we're happy to work with you as our pastor." I checked their history. Their last female pastor, Ida M. Hottel, served there 1916–1930. I guess that just proves what pastors have often suspected: churches have long memories.

Still, I know there are churches that still don't understand that God does pour out God's Spirit on all flesh and that whomever God calls, God sends to share the good news of God's mission to the world through Jesus Christ. If we reject because of gender or race or ethnicity one sent by God, if we fail to offer hospitality, we do so at the peril of our souls. We lose thereby the great joy of working with God as God stretches us to be more than we knew we could be in Christ Jesus, our Lord.

Even though we've not yet reached perfection, our past contains much to celebrate. The story of the Central Illinois Annual Conference is a moving one. From farm to factory, from river to hillside, from small town to city, the people now called United Methodist, once called evangelical, United Brethren, Evangelical United Brethren, Methodist Episcopal, and Methodist Protestants, and just plain old Methodist, have seen God's work among them in a mighty way. God has blessed and brought to fruition the labors of ministry. The harvest has been plentiful because the witnesses have been faithful.

Throughout this historic year, the members of the central and southern Illinois cabinets have worked as an area cabinet—one foot in the past, one foot in the future. Ever since that proposal at annual conference last year, when you invited the Southern Illinois Annual Conference to come and "get hitched," our lives have been enriched. Just as the months and days before a wedding are crazy and hectic, so has our year as a cabinet been: crazy with excitement and growth and challenge. Our oneness together as an area cabinet has been a joy. We've been part of the harmonious blend of folks from north and south of the line on the uniting conference task force. We've been heartened by reports from various commissions, boards, and committees who have held congenial joint meetings, where swift resolution of differing policies brought a single recommendation for our working together into the future.

The year has had the flavor of events I remember from my childhood: family reunions. I remember the family reunion when I was first introduced to cousins Peggy and Kenny. I knew they couldn't be kin of mine. They had *red* hair. They were tallish and skinny. They certainly couldn't be my kin. But by the time we had climbed to the forbidden heights of the corn crib to scoot, teetering across the topmost edge of the bin, trying not to fall either onto the hard-packed dirt floor on one side or into the suffocating corn on the other side, I knew we were kin after all. And by the time we'd kicked off our shoes and chased snakes down by the "crick," I couldn't remember a time when I'd not known them. And when the bully who lived down the road sauntered up to make mischief, we—together—took courage and chased him back down the road. Yes, I knew we were kin after all. Then I was mighty grateful for these members of my family, whom I'd not even known before.

That's how it's been to work with folks from the former Sothern Illinois Annual Conference: like discovering kin I hadn't even known I had. They speak our language, they share our dreams, they add fresh perspectives and new wisdom. And twelve of us have been able, by God's grace, to glimpse a broader perspective of God's vision for God's church than eight of us, or four of them, had been able to see. The larger appointment pool has offered greater opportunities for the gifts of clergy to be matched to the leadership needs of churches and clergy from one another's annual conferences. We have been pleased to find new (to us) clergy, whose gifts meet the needs of churches north of the fast-disappearing annual conference line.

This, too, is like those family reunions I remember. Everybody brought their gifts. Aunt Clara's bread and butter pickles vied with Cousin Dorothy's burnt sugar cake, and everyone else's best on a picnic table, which sagged under the luscious load. Uncle Ross's strong arm took the last turn of the crank of the ice cream freezer after us kids had all had our easy turns. Cousin Floyd brought stories old and new to share. Grandpa could throw a mean horseshoe, and Lula Mae always trotted out a fancy, new dress pattern she'd brought in the city for the women to "ooh" and "ahh" over. It was wonderful! Even Sandy, the cocker spaniel, entertained us by carefully burying the ice cubes she begged from our iced tea glasses, returning later to search for the ice cubes, racing frantically to and fro, trying to figure out where they'd gone.

The abundance of gifts being brought together is reality today just as it was then. What a rich treasure we now share and will share even more completely come August 17 and after. A veritable feast of gifts and abilities will be spread in the service of our God. The potential for catching and sharing a vision of what God is calling us toward in the future is great.

Our brothers and sisters from the former Southern Illinois Annual Conference bring their tradition of camp meetings, revivals, and evangelistic spirit. They bring the concept of clusters as a model for doing effective ministry. They bring determination and the gift of believing that whatever God calls us to do can be done. They bring to us the only rural Community of Shalom in the nation. They bring opportunities for ministry to one of the fastest changing and rapidly growing metro areas in the state. They bring yeast and salt and light.

What do we bring? We bring, too, yeast and salt and light, of course. We bring new church starts. We bring churches in transformation. We bring Communities of Shalom and hopes and dreams for a shalom world. We bring growing understanding, appreciation, and involvement in many models of cooperative ministries. We bring memories of the past and expertise for the cyberspace world of tomorrow. We bring courage to explore charge realignments, reexamination of our understanding of the mission of the church as a saving station doing ministry in and with its community. We bring the courage to stand up against the proliferation of gambling and racism and hate groups. We bring our strong faith in Jesus Christ and witness that God's love is an ark that can carry us through any flood or storm. We bring diversity of people and ministries and concerns, particularly for the Hispanic, Native Americans, and Korean among us.

What a bounteous offering we bring when we offer ourselves and our gifts on the table of the Lord. The table groans with the weight of it, especially when we add all our sisters and brothers from the Southern Illinois Annual Conference bring as well. From the perspective of the cabinet, we have been able to see this feast, which God has prepared for a world hungering and thirsting for salvation, for healing, for love. And it's going to be so great at the table together that we'll never again hear comments about serving iced tea with or without sugar. All the thirsty will find refreshment. All will be satisfied. Perhaps someday soon, iced tea will no longer be a symbol of difference and tensions but a reminder that God provides to all according to our needs and unites us according to the Spirit. Someday we will really celebrate out diversity as we work in unity. The cabinet is excited about the rich array of gifts, which will be brought together in one new annual conference, for the needs are many, and the needs of our future are not yet clearly known. Indeed, one of the issues before us this year has been the struggle to let God do a *new* thing among us. We've experienced the tension between wanting closure and wanting to leave space and time for God's Spirit to work among us. We've wanted to trust yet feared letting go. We've balked at structure and authority while fearing the chaos, which is necessary, before the new can emerge.

The cabinet has wrestled with other concerns and searched for solutions this past year. For example, we've been concerned with ministerial supply. Where are the clergy who will lead us tomorrow and into the twenty-first century? Clergy misconduct is another issue. How do we help clergy to grow strong spiritually and care for themselves so they are less vulnerable to the temptations that cause us to destroy our own lives and the lives of other individuals and the lives of congregations? There are the crying needs of the children and youth, who are part of our present and will be our future.

How do we as the church witness to and support parents in the difficult task of raising up children to the Lord? Giving our support to the bishop and Martha Lawson Endowed Scholarship for Africa University, which has the potential of changing the lives of thousands of children of Africa and around the world, is a tremendous opportunity to make a difference. Will we rise to the challenge before us? Another issue that is ever present for us as superintendents is this: how do we as superintendents find time away from the remedial, cleanup, supervisory work to give time to strong churches and effective pastors, who, with just a little more support and resourcing and encouragement, might be even stronger? And, of course, an issue for us this year is the issue that never goes away—the unfinished agenda of the "isms": racism, sexism, ageism. How do we deal with increasingly overt and violent manifestations of these sins in the world and even in our churches? The burning of black churches in the south, the KKK rallies within our annual conference, signs of hate among us. Where do we begin in the struggle to bring hating and hurting hearts to experience the healing love of Christ? Saints and sages planted seeds. God's Spirit moves among us, calling us to harvest the increase. God calls us out of our church buildings and into the mission field, which is the world. God calls us to spend more time with the unchurched to learn of their needs and to convince them that the church has something that will meet their deepest needs. God offers us the gift of discernment so we may know God's vision and God's mission through and purposes for the new annual conference.

What is our future? That is the question our area cabinet has been asking this year, even though we know by faith that even in midst of change, we are all right and will be all right because God is in it. We hear little whispers of doubt and quivers of fear in the people who want to know and don't want to know the answer. Some wonder whether they are going to lose their turf, their clout, their power, their place of honor at the table. Some wonder whether they will be invited in forgetting God is the host who invites all in. Some wonder whether their ministry concerns will continue to be concerns in the new annual conference. There is always tension when God is doing a new thing, and we don't quite know yet what it is.

Everything wasn't always peachy at our family reunions. Sadie always complained that whatever she brought just didn't turn out right, and Jeffie whined, and Sarah pouted because the necessary room was down a path instead of inside the house. Somebody always climbed the cherry tree and couldn't get back down. Uncle Max and Fred always discussed politics—*loudly*. Somebody always complained that the well water tasted funny. But none of that really mattered. There was always room at the table. We ate and laughed and played and talked, and it was wonderful. And when it was late and most of the folks had gone home, the big folks who were left would put us kids to bed up on Gramma's old feather bed. But we would try to stay awake and tiptoe over to the register in the floor and lie down and listen to the grown-ups gathered in the kitchen below. Up there, in the dark, the crowns of little red heads and blond heads and dark heads touched over the register in perfect silence at the wonder of grown-up things. We were kin. We were one in curiosity.

May we all be one in curiosity and faith and anticipation as we see the emerging vision of what God calls us to be. We needn't worry that our efforts, the ministries we've built, and the traditions we treasure will melt like the ice cubes our cocker spaniel buried on a hot summer day. Those folks south of I-70 are our kin. They treasure our gifts, our traditions, our faith as we treasure theirs.

"Unless a grain of wheat falls into the ground and dies," Jesus according to John tells us—unless the seed falls into the ground and dies—new life will not indeed, cannot, come forth (John 12:24 NRSV). We feel sadness that this Central Illinois Annual Conference will be no more except in memories, but we feel joyful anticipation of what new thing will spring forth. What is God already doing and inviting us to be a part of in the future? We wait and watch in hope and eager anticipation, like kids gathered around the register in the floor, seeking to see and to grasp the future—our future in God's future. And we have a special cause for rejoicing today as we work and wait, for we know our kin from the Sothern Illinois Annual Conference will soon be working with us. We are kin. We are one in curiosity about what is coming. Knowing there is work to be done, that there are souls to be won, how good it is to join together in our labors. May God bless us everyone as we prepare to harvest what the future brings. May God be glorified as we labor together for God!*

---

* Mary was the first woman to serve as chairperson of the Central Illinois Conference Cabinet. She delivered the cabinet address at the annual conference in 1996. This address was previously published in the *Central Illinois Annual Conference Journal*, 1996, pp. 489–494.

75

Loving the Child Within

Today I want to talk with you about child abuse and neglect and murder, etcetera. Lots of etcetera. Mostly I want to talk with you about the child within. Some of the questions we'll be considering are these: Who is the child within? Why can't we love the child? How do we learn to love the child? Who is the child within? This is an appropriate question, for many of us may be totally unacquainted with her. Let me introduce you. The child is a person full of wonder and of love and delight who enjoys learning a new hymn or two. The child is a collector—maybe not of bugs and snakes and rocks and other fascinating objects—but a collector of experiences. The child welcomes new experiences, such as attending Personal Growth Days and Schools of Christian Missions. The child is reaching, open, daring to be and to grow and to imagine. The child is creative—with a nonstop imagination and new ways of seeing old things.

She imagines, for example, what it would be like on this windy day if someone opened the front doors wide and the whole corps of district United Methodist Women officers were lifted by their large butterfly name tags and became airborne. She imagines, for example, how Bonnie Hensley broke her elbow. Bonnie was, I imagine, making a long shepherd's crook to use to haul speakers from the microphone if they tried to take more than their allotted three minutes today. The pole she was using was so long that she became tangled up in it and fell, breaking her elbow, skinning her knees, and inflicting immense damage to her dignity as well as to her body. The child is playful, spontaneous, and joyful ... which means the child is worshipping—naturally in tune with life or God, being responsive and responding to the holy.

Gertrude Mueller Nelson, in her book *To Dance with God: Family Ritual and Community Celebration*, tells of being busy with a sewing project when she noticed her three-year-old daughter's activities. The child, whose name is Annika, was busy pulling brightly colored strips of cloth, the trimmings from her mother's project, out of the wastebasket. Gertrude later found her daughter sitting in the grass in the backyard, fastening the strips of fabric to a long pole with wads of sticky tape. When Gertrude asked the child what she was doing, Annika explained, "I'm making a banner for a procession. I need a procession so that God will come down and dance with us."[5] Gertrude Mueller Nelson's story reminds us that the child erases the barriers *we* make between the holy and the everyday. When our human-made barricades and walls are removed, heaven comes down to dance with us in our ordinary lives. God called this incarnation. And the first child to make it happen was Mary.

In summary, then, *the child is the image of God in each of you.* This fetal being, created in the image of God, is the child God intends for you to love and nurture into full humanity, fullness of life. If this is true, why don't we fulfill God's purpose for us?

Why can't we love the child within? One reason is that somebody's playing "Wishbone" with us. Women are pulled in two—at least two—different directions. We are taught not to like ourselves and not to like other women. We are taught that "women's work," women's interests, women's skills, and women's way of looking at the world are wrong or silly or less important than men's. Women are taught that their value comes only from serving, from what we can do for others, denying our own needs, wants, self.

On the other hand, we are being taught that it's important to develop ourselves, to take care of ourselves, to become all we can be. Thus, we are pulled in two directions, like the wishbone.

Another reason we can't love the child within is that we are starving, abusing, and neglecting the child within because we are supposed to do everything for everybody else. This comes from our having been carefully taught that we have value and worth only if we *are good, so good, and look good!* Do you know how many millions of women have been tortured in panty girdles because of this warped value system? How many women's God-given gifts and graces, minds, and talents have been wasted because of this mindset?

In their book *Too Good for Her Own Good; Breaking Free from the Burden of Female Responsibility*, Claudia Bepko and Jo-Ann Krestan suggest that as women we are carefully taught the "woman's code of goodness" that lets us know in no uncertain terms that being good is knowing you are never good enough.[6] Good grief! No wonder depression is epidemic among women! No wonder we are confused, in pain, dissatisfied, and guilt ridden because we are dissatisfied. We are told that we have no cause for dissatisfaction, that we can have it all; we can have anything we want ... we just have to try harder. Since we are taught that our value comes only from caring for others, we must deny our own needs.

Yet at the same time, we are told, "If you don't take care of yourself, who will? You must take care of yourself so that you can take care of others." We think we don't measure up, yet we are taught that we should keep trying. And the harder we try, the higher the expectations placed on us, and the more the "all" becomes that we are supposed to be wanting and achieving. We are taught to want it all and expected to do it all ... *perfectly*! Whew! I get tired just thinking about it.

You may remember the popular poster of a decade or so ago that said something like, "When I finally get it all together, I'll probably forget where I put it." I've invented a statement I think is every woman's cry: "When I finally get it all together, I found out it wasn't enough."

Have you ever had that feeling? The feeling that you're trying to do everything for everybody, and you can't be the indispensable woman, so you feel like there is something wrong with *you* ... and in the meantime, the child inside you—that potentially playful, creative, joyful, dancing image of God—is shriveling up into a dried-out prune of a potential person instead of what she's supposed to be becoming.

Why do we need to love the child? The way we are trying to be and live is unhealthy for children and for other living things. We are guilty of child abuse and neglect; we are wasting ourselves in depression, in low functioning, in low self-esteem and self-doubt. We are wasting the talents of others by permitting them to be irresponsible, while we assume too much responsibility for the universe. This way of taking care of others when they should be taking care of themselves is called "codependency." If you don't know about it, read about it.

Why do we need to love the child within? Because you need to remember every day that your child is a precious gift, the most precious gift you will ever receive. To reject that gift is to reject the Giver. If you reject the gift, the *you* God made you to be—the child within you—and thus reject the Giver, you do so at the peril of your spiritual well-being.

Counselors who work with women report that many of their clients complain of a hollowness, an emptiness, a sense that "there's nobody in here." This is because our child is dying, and we don't know what to do; we may not even know that we *need* to do something. The God-shaped hole that can be filled only by nurturing a growing spiritual relationship with Jesus Christ is empty if we don't nourish that child, that image of God, within us.

Because our compulsive duty-ridden behavior produces resentment and anger, and brings death to the child, we aren't free to love God and others. We must be freed to laugh and sing, to enjoy and experience if we are to dance with God. We cannot be free to love others when we feel enslaved, burdened with responsibility and duty. No wonder our child is crying: she's feeling smothered.

If you want to be a butterfly, you need to ditch the cocoon, the cocoon of mindless, unexamined duty, and let fear and self-doubt go. Nobody's sitting on your chrysalis but your own fear and doubt. Fly free; be at peace with yourself. Love yourself as a precious child of God.

When we are at peace with ourselves, we find it easy to love others and to value them as persons ... as we are called to do. When we are comfortable with ourselves, we can be comfortable with others. We can be open, honest, and accepting.

If, on the other hand, we dislike ourselves, we may turn our self-criticism outward. The loving, accepting child is sent to her room, and she shrivels up in shame. Then she may become angry and kick the cat or fuss with her brother. Or maybe she turns her anger inward and becomes depressed. Wherever the anger goes, it hurts the child and her relationships.

We need to love the child in here so we can love and serve the little ones out there. We are United Methodist Women. We have a long tradition of caring for the least and lost, the powerless and marginalized. We willingly take up our responsibility to continue that tradition. But if we are to do so with joy, with full empowerment, we must love the child within, and let that child within grow and live, and laugh and weep with the children of the world. Then our work for justice will be more than duty; it will be a joyful dance for service to our God.

We need to love the child within so we can model healthy caring—caring that nurtures us and others "to empower freedom as whole persons through Jesus Christ," as we state in our purpose.

We need to nurture the child within so we can develop confidence in our decision-making skills. We need to use our power in the broader area, becoming involved in decisions at the policy-making level rather than just cleaning up the messes left by those who make decisions based on greed and lust for power. Women need to say, as a T-shirt I saw recently so eloquently put it, "Mother-Earth says, 'Clean up your room!'" Above all, we must model self-esteem for the coming generations, who are just learning what it means to be a woman. We must show them the healthy, worshipping way of life that tears away the barriers between earth and heaven and gives sanctity and importance to all we do. We must break the cycle of child abuse and neglect by caring for our own child within and teaching our daughters to do so as well. When we are convinced of our self-worth as children of God, we will come to honor others too much to do harm. When we break the cycle of oppression and devaluation upon which we embark when we are born women, we will esteem others more highly.

Remember, when we nurture our child within, we are honoring the image of God within us. We are becoming the person God wants us to be. Instead of quenching the Spirit, we are inviting the Spirit to empower us to live and serve as God has created us to do.

So, how do we learn to love the child? First, we become aware that someone is playing "wishbone" with us, and we choose to pull ourselves free of those who would pull us this way and that. We choose, intentionally and fully informed, to find the unique way of living and the path of serving to which each of us is called, which honors who we are and recognizes our gifts. We understand that it's okay to care for ourselves and for others and to choose how and when we shall do each.

Second, we stop "should-ing" on ourselves. We dump the code of goodness that says our only value comes from being good, doing good, and looking good. Instead, we accept that it is our status as God's precious children that gives us our worth. It is our relationship with God, which we haven't earned and cannot buy, that gives us value. We are a sister of Christ, who loved us completely, who, when he walked among us as Jesus of Nazareth, treated women with honor and respect. He treated women as if they had minds and feelings and dignity and worth.

I recently called on a parishioner who was dying of cancer. Also present in her home that day was the wife of her husband's minister; his lovely lady seemed to me to be the epitome of what United Methodist

Women are not. Her smile seemed to have died long years ago. Judging from the tightness of her corset, I suspect the child was strangled by spandex.

Tragically, the mind of this poor minister's wife was apparently turned into some mindless recording device. In the course of her conversation, she had numerous opportunities to say, "Well, I think" or "This is what I believe" or "I wonder" or even "I wish." Instead, her comments during the entire conversation were all prefaced with, "Pastor says ..."

I grieved for this poor woman. Though to tell you the honest truth, it was all I could do to keep my child from asking her, "But what do *you* think?" and "What do *you* say?" But my child honored the sad, empty shell of the good Christian lady too much to ask. Instead, I just grieved for her dead child. I also prayed that she didn't have any daughters and didn't teach any girls in Sunday school.

How do we learn to love the child? We restore the balance of our lives. We spend time being—being in the presence of God and being present to others—not trying to be the source of all wisdom and truth and help but being there as Christ was truly present to the women he met in his earthly ministry and as he is present with us today. You love your child only by taking up the responsibility that is rightfully yours. You remember that God didn't die and leave you in charge of the universe. You share responsibility with others, encouraging them to find their own solutions, thus teaching them that they are capable and strong, and that with God's help, they can grow toward solutions to their own concerns. The first thing I learned from United Methodist Women was what it means to be in mission. We minister with; we are in mission *with* persons, not Ms. Fix-its for everybody. We honor the wisdom of others when they say, "This is how you can help me" or "This is what I need from you" rather than telling others, "This is what you need. This is what you really want." Women know only too well what it is like to be told that their feelings or desires are wrong. Thus, we can be sensitive to the need of others to discover for themselves what they want and need, and we can honor their child within, the truth the Spirit of God teaches them.

Finally, if we are to love the child within, we must kill the "Angel in the House." In 1981, a well-known female writer was trying to explain to a group of women how, even though her profession wasn't officially or even unofficially barred to women, other powerful forces had made it exceedingly difficult for her to practice her chosen profession, which she began as a reviewer of books.

While I was writing my first review, I discovered that that if I were going to review books, I should need to do battle with a certain phantom ... a woman who when I came to know her better, I called, "The Angel in the House." It was she who used to come between me and my paper when I was writing reviews. It was she who bothered me and wasted my time and so tormented me that at last I killed her. I will describe her as shortly as I can. She was intensely sympathetic. She was immensely charming. She sacrificed herself daily ... she never had a mind or wish of her own." " ...when (ever) I came to write, I encountered her with the very first words. The shadow of her wings fell on my page; I heard the rustling of her skirts in the room ... I took my pen in my hand to review that novel by a famous man; she slipped behind me and whispered, 'My dear, you are a young woman. You are writing about a book that has been written by a man. Be sympathetic; be tender; flatter; deceive; use all the arts and wiles of your sex. Never let anybody know that you guess that you have a mind of your own. Above all, be pure. And she made as if to guide my pen. "I now record the one act for which I take some credit to myself, though the credit rightly belongs to some excellent ancestors of mine who left me a certain sum of money ... so that it was not necessary for me to depend solely on charm for my living. I turned upon her and caught her by the throat. I did my best to kill her. My excuse, if I were to be (charged) in a court of law, would be that I acted in self-defense. Had I not killed her, she would have killed me. She would have plucked the heart out of my writing. Thus, whenever I felt the shadow of her wing or the radiance of her halo, I took up the inkpot and flung it at her. It is far harder to kill a phantom than a reality."[7]

Karen Payne, editor of *Between Ourselves: Letters Between Mothers and Daughters*, from whose book the above quote comes, adds, "[More than] fifty years later the specter of the angel in the house [has] not completely lost its grip on popular notions of womanhood." Yes, there are still phantoms that would encourage you to kill the child within you so that you are a "good" woman. But good women know they are called by Jesus Christ to grow into women who are strong and are aware of the child within. These women know they are called by the risen Christ to *life*—full and abundant life. And the goals we have as United Methodist women come out of that call to live to encourage and enable to live fully also. We've been warned from the cradle against the sin of pride, but women's sin isn't pride; it's self-abnegation—which, simply stated, is abusing, neglecting, and/or murdering the child within. The healthy pride of loving the child within is not sin. It is the will and work of God. Love the child within. She is your best self, the child God means you to be. The child called to dance and sing and laugh and weep in worshipful praise of her Creator. Love the child within so she can be a sign of hope for other children, not yet set free from the angel in the house.

Let us pray: O God, help us to love ourselves in healthy ways so we may love others freely and fully without anger or resentment. Help us to nurture and care for the child within so we may nurture others toward strength and wholeness and self-responsibility. Help us, O gracious Giver of life, to love the child within—your gift to us—so we may dance with you, cocreating justice and righteousness and joy in our world. In the name of the risen Christ, even Jesus of Nazareth, who during his life on earth showed women respect and honor, thus showing us how we are to live with ourselves and one another, we pray. Amen.*

---

* Mary gave this speech before the Galesburg District United Methodist Women's Meeting, April 9, 1991, at the Knoxville United Methodist Church, Knoxville, Illinois.

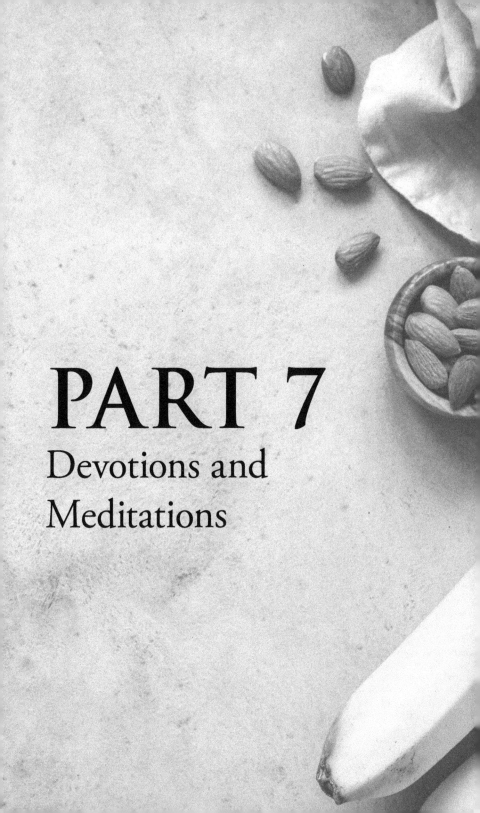

PART 7
Devotions and Meditations

76

Starfish

Scripture, Tradition, Experience, Reason

A starfish dreamed in the bottom of the sea. She was wonderfully graceful and orange, and covered with artful lumps. A thing of beauty, she swam alone in the depths of the sea. The song of the surge soothed her ears, and life was good. One day as the starfish floated among the coral, tickled by the playful wavelets, a great school of fish swam around her.

"We are going in search of truth," they bubbled. "Pray give us one of your legs that with experience we may find wisdom."

The starfish permitted her leg to be broken off, and the fish swam away. The starfish floated only a little wobbly. The surf song was gentle, and life was good.

A second day as the starfish floated in the warm sea, the great school of fish returned. "Pray give us another of your legs, good starfish," they begged. "We go in search of truth and need a pointer to mark our place in the Great Book!"

The starfish permitted a second leg to be removed, and the fish swam away, leaving the wobbly starfish to be tossed by the surge. But the sea's song was gentle, and life was good.

On yet another day, the starfish wobbled in the warm sea, and the great school of fish returned to beg, "Dear starfish, we go in search of truth today, and tradition says that we must take one of your legs with us. Pray permit us to take it quietly that we may honor tradition." The starfish assented and was left floundering in the surf, helpless to direct her path. The sea's song was wilder that day, but life was good.

On yet another day, the fish came to where the starfish wobbled in the ocean depths. "Come, give us another leg," the fish called. "Surely with your leg to scratch our heads with, we may reason out truth."

The weary starfish assented, and the fish swam away, leaving the starfish on her last leg. She sank slowly to the bottom of the sea. And floated out at the whim of the waves and tides, sometimes tossed and scraped on the coral, her dream-filled sleep.

Finally, a day came when the song grew so loud that the starfish could sleep no more. She loosened her grip on the coral, prepared to float helplessly away. But as is the way of starfish, she had grown new legs. She was whole and balanced. She could once again propel herself through the sunlit waves. The starfish cavorted in the surf, and life was good.

As the starfish drifted, delighted with her new freedom, the great school of fish returned and cried, "Starfish, we go in search of truth. Give us one of your legs to help us."

The starfish paused for a moment, feeling the soft, warm water lap gently against her restored, balanced self. The song of the sea called more loudly, still wonderfully graceful presence, orange, and artfully lumpy.

"Yes," said the starfish. "Helping is what starfishes are about." The song of the sea growing louder, the melody drowning the roar of the waves breaking on rocks. But only the music was heard; no words were left unsaid.

The great shimmering school of fish surrounded the starfish. They gazed at her balance. "We have found truth," they bubbled. And life was very good, for it is in giving that we receive.

77

Turn Not Thy Face

The Mormons do it well; the panorama of faces—brown, black, yellow, red, white—drifts across the screen. Wordless, the scene hooks you until the words come. "If you can't see God here, you probably won't see God at all."

What does God look like? Like those faces flickering across the television screen? Is it true that if we don't see God in others, we won't see God anywhere? Do we not see God there because we won't?

The psalmist pleads with God not to turn the divine countenance away. But instead of God's turning face, maybe we turn our faces.

I never understood what the psalmist was talking about until I met John and the big jars. It was during rehearsals for a musical murder mystery I was directing. The set design called for two large ceramic jars. Somebody had seen them in front of a house up the road. With trepidation I told one of the cast to go ahead and ask her neighbor if we could use them. On the second night of rehearsal, John broke one. I was upset, especially since he'd been horsing around when it happened. I was too upset to speak with him about it, so I turned my face from him and walked away. Later, when I had cooled down and went to talk to him, John was crushed. He was shriveled up into a hurting teenager. "Why didn't you yell at me?" he asked. "Why didn't you scream at me or cuss me out or sock me? I could have stood that but … but you wouldn't even look at me. I couldn't stand that!"

Turn not thy face from me … sometimes we turn from others or from God in anger, pain, or fear. Like the child who won't look her questioning parent in the eye because the parent can read guilt there, we don't look at God. Sometimes we are just totally distracted by things that are much less important.

Emily is the young woman in the play *Our Town* by Thornton Wilder; she dies in childbirth. As she lingers in that undesignated place where all the dead are gathered on stage, she asks to go back. The others try to dissuade her. She insists. "Well, then tell her, 'If you must go back, pick an ordinary day.'" But Emily chooses to go back on her fourteenth birthday. She is horrified to see how members of her family relate.

"Look at me, Momma," Emily pleads when her busy mother doesn't listen to the young woman's worries. When she returns to her place among the dead, Emily says, "Live people don't look at each other, do they? They don't really notice one another."

When we don't see others, we don't see God. Turn not your face away ... rather, turn and seek God.[*]

---

[*] Mary gave this as a devotion for the cabinet on Wednesday, May 20, 1998.

78

Bent Over but Looking Up

(Retell Luke 13:10–13.)

The woman had been bent over for years. What was that like? Bend over. What do you see? What do you not see? You miss out on much. How does that feel?

We don't know what made that woman bent over, but we know what makes us bent over: discouragement, worry, fear, burdens for others, disappointment. But we do know that things were about to start looking up for her. Jesus healed the woman; he went to her. He spoke to her. He addressed her with concern and respect. He touched her.

Jesus comes to you, who are bent over with cares. Jesus calls to you. Will you be healed of your burdens? Lay them on Jesus. Say, "Jesus, I trust you to care for me. I lay my burdens down and ask that you will heal me of fear, doubt, disappointment, worry." Even when we are bent over, things can start looking up for us. The woman who had been bent over and was immediately healed when Jesus touched her looked up. She praised God. And so should we all when God gives us strength to deal with our afflictions in life. That's the only way our lives can look up when we are bent over with concerns.

Let us look up and praise God for the love God showers on us.

One of the ways we can look up and praise God is to look around for those who are bent over with worry, with cares, with burdens that seem too heavy to bear. And touch them. Help those who are bent over to start looking up. You can call them, write to them, or speak to them in the corridor, or go down to their room and say, "I was just wondering how you are." And you can look up to God and pray for them. And maybe your sharing of God's love will help them to be able to straighten up under their burdens and give praise to God.

Let us pray: O God, sometimes our burdens of aging and aches and pains and worries about money and our families and our friends and our fading vision or memory almost bend us double with the weight of it all. But we thank you that you are a God who shares our burdens, who cares for us and wants us to look up to the hills from whence our help comes and to praise you and be glad. Help us to do that, Lord. We pray in the name of Jesus, who took away our burden of sin and cleanses us from all unrighteousness so we can cast off our shame and look up to you. For him, our light and our salvation, we give you thanks and praise. Amen.

79

A Guided Meditation

You awaken in darkness. As you gradually float into consciousness, you know you are in your own bed and that it is morning. And you are unwell. As you become more alert, you feel a nagging sense of being less than whole, of being "dis-eased." You get out of bed, moving gently, mentally taking inventory of how you feel everywhere. As you dress, you become aware of the location of whatever is wrong. You focus on that location and feel pain. You continue dressing in jeans, a comfortable shirt, and socks and shoes. Though you move slowly and feel de-energized, you are soon dressed. Pulling a jacket from the closet, you go out into the new day and walk toward a nearby woods. The sun flickers through the tall trees. Bird calls sound from the branches. Beneath your feet, the soft, moist earth yields gently to each step. The fallen pine needles form a fragrant soft carpet silencing your tread. You wander among the trees for a while, still with a sense of not being totally well, of not fully savoring the beauty of the morning.

In the distance, you glimpse a figure walking before you. You quicken your steps as some great yearning to catch him overcomes you. As he steps into the clearing, the full radiance of the morning sun falls on him; his whole figure seems filled with light. You gasp and almost stumble, for something tells you it is he, the Christ, the Great Physician, who walks before you. You quicken your pace still more, and just as you fear he will disappear into the dim forest beyond, he turns, and the full power of his gaze falls on you. You are shocked into stillness until he beckons you to join him. You approach his side and wander with him through the woods, through clearings, over fallen trees, and across laughing brooks. The birdsong is sweeter, the sun is warmer, the sky incredibly blue, the air soft and fragrant with pine and joy.

You forget your pain, your unwellness, as you wander with him, observing as he inspects the meadow grass in clearings, the shady spots beneath the tall trees, the banks of the streams, occasionally stooping to harvest an herb or flower or plant. By the time the sun is high overhead, you have gone a long way together. He stops beside a rushing stream and motions for you to rest on a smooth, sun-warmed boulder. He dips some of the icy water from the stream and prepares a tea of some of the plants he has collected. When it is ready, he offers you a drink. It is bitter and sweet, spicy and musky, and wonderful.

Lolling in the sunlight, perfectly serene and peaceful, you grow drowsy and lie down on a bed of soft pine needles and fall asleep. When you awaken, you are alone. The Great Physician is gone. You are alone ... except for your pain. Your pain is still with you. You are rested, still feeling the joy of the time spent in his presence, but the pain is the constant baseline to the melody of your afternoon.

You see the plants he had gathered still lying where he placed them. You gather them, seeing that the sun is low in the sky, and you head toward home, not so wearily, but puzzled that the pain remains. But your step is lighter, and the world seems brighter and more beautiful than before. You move with certainty, the herbs and plants nestled in your arms. At last, you emerge from the woods and see across the meadow your home. You hasten toward your private place in the world. The light of the setting sun bathes the windows with a crimson glow, and you hurry faster until you have approached quite near. Then you stop suddenly in surprise. Waiting for you are the other members of this group. They seem to anticipate your coming with hope, as if you had something for them.

Puzzled, you enter your home, motioning them to follow you. They gather with you around your kitchen table as you lay the herbs and plants on the table. Soon you have a large pot of water steaming on the stove and mugs for each guest and yourself on the table. Soon you place the herbs and plants in the boiling water, and the aroma of spice, bitterness, joy, and musky, mysterious tea fills the room. You ladle out the steaming brew into the cups before each friend and gaze around at their expectant faces. As they look at you, you feel that you want to offer a toast or a blessing. But you don't at first know what you have to offer them. You still feel your own pain. How can you offer healing to another?

Then you remember the presence with whom you walked in the

morning light. You remember how you forgot your pain for a moment, how you tasted joy in the fresh air, how you heard joy in the birdsong. How whole you had felt in spite of your "un-wholeness." And a sense of the same presence comes to you here in this room, filled with members of the group and the scent of tea. And you bow your head as words come to you: "For all that we are, thanks. For all that may yet be, hope. For what we are not, grace. For what we are becoming together, patience. Amen."

As the scene softly fades into memory, become gradually aware of the here and now, of the presence of others with you, of the fragrance of gifts given and received, of the continuing pain within and among, as, like tree branches in the wind, we scrape against one another. Awake and be at peace. Amen.

80

Meditation on a Dream Symbol

Close eyes.

Get in touch with breathing.

Notice body sensations … travel around the body … relax tense muscles.

Continue to quiet and center self in any way that works for you.

Now bring into focus before you a dream symbol … place it in front of you in any way you desire. Walk around it in your mind's eye and explore its uniqueness … notice its size … shape … colors … textures … any smell … touch it if you wish … touch it to parts of your body if you would like to do so.

Now look once more at all the various details of your symbol …

Place it back in front of you … Begin to speak to it … Ask it questions about itself … its life, its origin … its future … Listen while it unfolds to you the secret of its being and of its destiny …

Listen while it explains to you what existence in your dream means to it …

Your symbol has some hidden wisdom to reveal to you about yourself …

Ask for this wisdom and see what the symbol has to say …

There is something you can give this symbol. What is it? What does it want from you? …

Now place yourself and your symbol in the presence of Jesus Christ. Listen to what he has to say to you and the symbol. What do the two of you say in response?

Now it is time to leave the symbol. Say any words of parting that you wish, knowing you may return to them at any time …

Slowly bring your awareness back to the room …

As you feel ready, open your eyes and rejoin the group.

81

A Directed Imagery
Experience on Worship

Relax. Move back in memory, back in time to a moment when worship really happened for you. A moment when you almost expected to hear the voice of God say, "Take off your shoes; you are on holy ground." Go back to a worship experience when you felt powerfully the presence of God, when you were inspired and moved ...

Where were you? How does that worship begin? Follow the activities of that worship experience as they flow through time. Notice sounds ... music? Singing? Praying? Preaching? What images came to your mind as you worshipped in that special moment? What feelings did you experience?

Follow through the experience until it comes to an end. What activities brought it to a close? How did you feel as worship closes and you went forth? What did you take away from the time that is still special to you ... memories? Feelings? Hopes for future worship experiences?

Take a moment to thank God for that special worship time. Thank God for being present with you. Seek assurance that the divine presence will be with you in future moments. Amen.

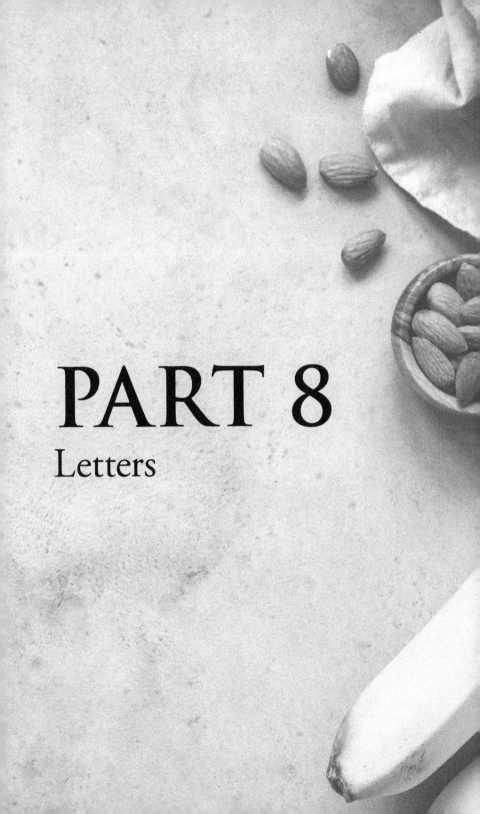

PART 8

Letters

82

Ministry in the Rural Setting

Dear Pastor:

Thank you for taking my first letter in the spirit in which I'd intended it and for inviting me to help you, as I said, "recognize the basic values" of this parish. I am very happy to do just that.

First of all, you might find it helpful to recognize that what we do in our micro society is "normal" to us. When you try to change us, we feel that you are implying we are wrong. We have our norms; our values will remain after you are gone. You can teach us that God loves us if you love us as we are. Then we may be free to change as you believe we should. But we will choose what is viable and good for us. Do not cut and stretch us to fit the box given you by the Big Church. Cut and fit the demands of the Big Church to fit us. On the other hand, we are proud when we can grow and meet some expectations of the Big Church. When we "don't measure up," we may be ashamed and embarrassed. We have our pride, you know. Then we may become angry with you, Big Church's representative to us. Please don't humiliate us. Help us through our ambiguous feelings to feel worthy. After all, we do change ultimately, but our measuring sticks and clocks are our own. Learn to translate from your English system to our metric system; learn to translate from your White-Rabbit Time to our Eternal Hills Time. Look at us carefully; we have a culture. We have our own dreams. We have our visions. Bring yours to us as other visions, other dreams, not as "The Vision, The Dream." Show us what value lies for us in your dreams, and we will listen. And through listening we will come to understand and trust you more. We may not change, but we will understand your perspective better. We believe "small is beautiful," and our values revolve around that.

Understand that our taboos are part of us. We strive to live by our moral code. But we protect those of our "family" who fail to do so. Our super ego is alive and well, and we are afraid that immorality may come in from "outside" and subvert us. That is one reason we fear change. We don't really value spontaneity; licentiousness is unacceptable, for it would destroy our world. "Do what feels good" is not a philosophy we could live with because we would lose our means of controlling how things are here.

When someone from outside—like a minister—tells us we have already been invaded and subverted, we become angry and fearful. Our anger is often misplaced on the teller. If you will accept our anger and gently lead us to remember how we were before the invasion, we will come to realize how we have been changed. We might even see that we have survived change. But we will also be even more distrustful and fearful of change.

That is our fear source, you know; the world impinges on us, would engulf us, destroying our unique identity. We feel helpless in our smallness. Our feeling vulnerable makes us more defensive. Small armies need higher walls. Only when we have watched carefully the one who approaches and have seen that the stranger walks on two feet like unto ourselves will we permit the new one to come into where we live. If you don't betray us, we will show you what "family" means. We like our privacy, Pastor. We don't let strangers in easily if they have come to stare at the "hicks" and laugh. But in our own time we may choose to welcome you.

Let us then discover one another. Who are *you*, Pastor? Why do you care for us? Do you care for *us* or for some image you have of who you imagine us to be? Will you try to force us to change? Will you use us to satisfy your needs? Will you want to rip away stones from the very foundation of our walls before you check to see what they support? You need not ask us what they support, for we too live partly unexamined lives. That is why we dream at night, so that we may not be blinded by too much truth. If you try to pry open our eyes, we will fight you. Sometimes for us it is enough to say no to change, to say only, "We've always done it this way."

Do not scorn us because we are enfolded in the arms of Grandmother Tradition. To be thus does not necessarily mean we still suck our thumbs. Those arms are a safe place from which to watch and rest until we choose to leave her arms and change.

Pastor, we treasure our rites of passage. We will smile tolerantly if you speak of "infant baptism," but when we all show up on Sunday, we know that it is because Amy Jo and Clyde Carl are having their baby christened. We won't confront you on such issues, but we are pretty good at passive resistance. We'd really rather not talk about some issues upon which we disagree. We respect your role, and after all, less said, sooner mended. But we'd like you to understand what our silences say.

In our family parish, we see all stages of development, and our security comes in part in the predictableness of how it will be for us along the flow of life. When you share in our rites, such as our annual homecoming, and listen as we tell you who died since last year, you are more a part of us than you know. You help us feel that God is with us through the years. We are frightened when our young people must move away for economic reasons, thus causing us to miss watching their children develop. And we have a sense that rites of passage are authentic only when they occur here. Invite us to talk of those children and grandchildren, Pastor, with or without photographs, for doing so makes them real for us, and they are our future.

Our human needs are generally the same as those of persons everywhere. Yet each of us has unique concerns. You can provide pastoral care for us best by observing how we meet individual needs. Even if you don't see how we can be content with what we have, respect our knowing what we need. Perhaps we are more "self-actualized," as you call it, than we appear to you. Our lifestyles are generally constructive. We protect those of us who turn to destructive patterns as much as we can. Once in a while, we lose one of us to suicide, and you can be sure the whole town gets mighty thoughtful for a while. We would especially need you then, Pastor, to help us forgive ourselves for not being enough for the lost one. Care for us as we care for one another, but don't expect us to tell you our deepest concerns the first time you call on us. If you have seen one of us, we will reveal who we are and what pains us.

If you would be our pastor, see us as individuals. I suspect that you have encountered us as a group, and since we don't flaunt our individuality, you will need to search out what each of us values in himself or herself. For example, remember to compliment Zula Compton on her lime pickles at the potluck and ask Rosalie Huffman how her quilting is coming. Their special skills, whether they seem impressive to you or not, are their means of recognition among us. When we compliment Zula, we say, "We value your contribution; we value you." See our unique needs; try to remember to ask how we are doing at our particular edge of pain. We find it easier to share if your remembering gives us the sense that you care. And in our telling our pain, the fear and loneliness recede.

You'd best attend to our weaknesses as well as our gifts. For example, don't forget to ask Annabelle how her latest X-rays came out (she spent the years since her husband died waiting for a recurrence of her cancer). And don't forget the anniversary of deaths. We remember and mourn annually. Don't be intimidated by Norma's hostility. She's been afraid of life ever since her father died and left her to care for her mother. Don't take any of our defenses personally, Pastor. Please recognize that some of us protect ourselves by being "formal." If you can avoid judging us as "cold" or "hung up" or "unfriendly," you may discover how to permit us to let you relate comfortably to us. Generally, our individual life spaces are large because we are few and live so close to one another. Thus, we have a protection in our bubbles, which prevents constant intimacy. Our pain is real, Pastor, even if some of our ways of dealing with our pain seem unreal to you.

I hope I shall not embarrass you if I mention that you, as the sole *new* person in our small town, are being scrutinized. If you can be increasingly real with us, we will care for you in your weaknesses as you will care for us. Just be natural with us and don't imagine that we are ignorant and uneducated. We know much of what is going on in the rest of the world, even if we don't choose to live elsewhere and even though we interpret everything from our village-centered perspective. Much of what we know "out there" seems strange and wrong and threatening, so we may prefer to talk about what is happening here. When we talk negatively about the world out there, we are not expressing a "sour-grapes" attitude, nor when we defend here (if we do so other than in silence) are we extolling a "sweet lemon." We don't want to be "there," and for the most part, we like our "here."

We don't always do as well as you think we should, but we do as well as we can or choose to do. Do not be ashamed of us or of yourself as pastor if we don't fulfill your expectations. We choose. If you can continue to love us in spite of ourselves, your caring will, in ways we don't really comprehend, permit us to grow. And you may come to understand that it is often right that we don't fulfill your expectations. Oddly, you as pastor are both parent or authority figure and child being socialized into our culture. If you can shift flexibly and patiently from one role to another, we can and will work with you. We will accept that you are doing the best you can for us. Most of us won't make you the scapegoat for the church's financial woes. And we will likely not go anywhere if we become angry with you. This is our ancestral, spiritual home. If anyone leaves our church, it is his or her choice anyway. No recriminations, please.

I hope that by now you have recognized that the myth of the peaceful, bucolic, Carnation-Contented-Cow rural world *is* a myth. I hope you have begun to perceive the stresses present in our lives. You have noticed the tension in Dan Murphy, haven't you? He is next in line to be laid off (the recession touches us, too). And Virgil Norman's strained silence is due to the bank's making foreclosure noises. When the price of combines is in the mid-five-digit range and a dry summer means farmers didn't make enough to pay for their seed and fertilizer, farmers are under considerable stress. You can care for us best by coming to know about such realities. Listen to Virgil tell about his granddaddy clearing that land and hear his fear of losing his home place, his roots. Hear the meaning beneath the words, Pastor. And then there is Marge. Her daughter has a "libber." Got a big job and her own secretary at the bank in town. Talks about her career but not about marriage and kids. Marge is afraid she will never have a grandbaby around. And this new lifestyle is a real stressor on our women. Marge is both proud of and disappointed by her "successful/failure" daughter. And who knows what guilt the daughter is feeling for breaking out of the role we accept?

You will probably notice other ways we react to stress, such as Vera's arthritis, which acts up when you don't call on her often enough. Folks know Vera; just smile and give her an extra call. We have our psychosomatic aches and pains. Love us anyway, and we will get better until the stress piles up again. It may take less life change to "get to" us than folks in the city can handle. But we do have a support group here. We cope by being "family" to one another. Caring for us means providing outlets through the church for us to de-stress. As you have observed, we do this pretty well already, but sometimes we miss someone. And you, Pastor, are looking a might peaked yourself. You can care for us best if you care for yourself. I suspect that some of your resources for coping were left back in the city. Take care. If you succumb to the Super Shepherd Syndrome, who will feed the sheep? But we do like for you to notice our particular stresses, such as illness or hospitalization, or moving someone to a nursing home. We have so much guilt about that, being so family oriented. When our extended-family value impacts a changing culture, we have much pain. Comfort us; help us believe we aren't bad people if we don't keep Granny at our house. Or help us believe we have the resources to keep Granny with us.

Both you and the people of the parish are conditioned to respond to life events. Our ways may differ from yours, just as there are differences among people of our congregation. The conditioning means our responses control us insofar as we are unaware of what is happening. Together we may examine processes that are occurring and enrich one another's understanding. Know what is pulling your stings and help us to see what is pulling ours. Since you are the only newcomer, your vision may be fresh enough to notice these processes. But be kind or gently confrontive as you articulate your observations.

We have expectations of you based on our value system. We expect our pastor to be modest, temperate, pious, kind of a saintly eunuch. We will permit you to pastor as you can, to some extent, fit the box we have for you. We will tolerate discrepancies increasingly as we come to know you *if* you don't brazenly do violence to all our mold. This probably seems manifestly unfair to you; remember, in a small town everyone knows who you are. Please don't embarrass us by behaving inappropriately in front of others. When we have come to love you, we will come to smile at some of your idiosyncrasies and defend you. It may be unfair, but we have very definite role expectations, and you are a public person. Some things are just not negotiable; humor us for a while until we stop noticing you so much. Then you will become as nearly one of us as anyone can, and then we will let you be *our* pastor.

You've probably noticed that we aren't exactly a pluralistic mini society. And you've probably noticed as well that we have very traditional views on marriage and sexuality here. Marriage is the norm. Some of us pretend we want to stay married because divorce is less accepted here than in the larger world. Singleness is an acceptable, but less valued, lifestyle. We just think people should be married. Yes, Pastor, we have heard that some psychologists say that "shoulding on yourself" isn't healthy, but that is the way we keep our mini society from changing. And, of course, we think married folks should have children. And heterosexual relationships are all that are acceptable here. For any other idea, one must go elsewhere. We certainly don't talk about homosexuality comfortably and are angry that our church is talking about homosexuality and abortions as possible options. We are so angry about this that we aren't really sure what the issues are. You might be able to help us hear—later. We would prefer just as soon that our kids didn't hear such talk, so I hope you aren't even considering any modern church school literature for your junior and senior highs. You'd raise a real hornets' nest with that! If you want to pastor us, you might as well know what we don't consider options. And you know that those who chose one of our non-options would be taking a lot of guilt with them. I guess their families would be pretty broken up if such as that happened. We seem so black and white on these issues (sin is sin) that such families would have no one to turn to in their grief and shame.

We do tend to control behavior here by ostracizing those who don't live according to the mold we make. That means we all watch ourselves closely. We have definite ideas about what are appropriate male and female roles, for example. You might help us give ourselves permission to affirm the whole male-and-female role of ourselves. We tend to hide a good part of ourselves and feel guilty when we don't want to hide it. As you probably can imagine, such hiding certainly limits our freedom to be spontaneous. Help us to be forgiving when we want to throw stones; help us to forgive ourselves for killing parts of us and others.

Some of our former pastors never could get the hang of our language. If you would be our pastor, you need to hear us accurately. I know listening is hard work, but we need that from you. To be heard is healing for us. We can forgive almost anything else of our pastor if he or she hears our spoken and silent language, our words and meanings. You might learn about us by listening to our local legends and even hearing us speak of the television shows we watch, the movies and books we enjoyed or disliked. Listen to such talk not as factual reviews but as it reveals what our heroes (and demons) are like. They can live the behaviors we deny ourselves. Upon them we can heap the emotional responses we prevent ourselves from directing on real people.

When we, a relatively immobile mini society, tell and recall our myths, we tell you who we are and reaffirm that our roots go back several generations. Retelling is like weaving a new strand into an old rope to strengthen it. When we tell "our stories," we let you into our innermost "family" world. We reveal what is most us. You will forgive the inaccuracies of our oral tradition. Sometimes we need to "remember things" differently than they were. To confront our embroidery would be even more rude than telling Zula Compton that her pickles are mushy or Virgil Norman that the days of the family farm are over. We expect you to be an adult, Pastor, and here the adults pretend the handicapped are whole until the disabled person indicates otherwise. When you accept an adult role with us, we can more easily mention our warts and paralysis—in our own time. Strangely, we are more honest about some things than is the larger society. One such subject is death; we seem to do less pretending that there's no such thing. Maybe the reason for our honesty is that we are close enough as one family in our town for a long time to really notice folks coming and going.

Pastor, I am gratified that you want to know more about us so you can help us. Wouldn't you be surprised to discover that we had helped one another? If you are like most pastors, you must have come to us imagining that you would change us. I suspect that the impact of our parish on you will be equally forceful. What happens here for you and for us may not be what any of us expected. However, if we listen to one another, we may all grow.*

Sincerely yours,
Mary Walsh

---

* Mary wrote this letter to fulfill a requirement for her Pastoral Care Class at Garrett Seminary.

83

A Letter from Mary

September 28, 1989

Dear Sheep of His Pasture, Tendril on the Vine,

I was deeply concerned yesterday as I saw the depth of your frustration, hurt, anger—almost despair —at the apparent unresponsiveness of the church (or the Church) to several concerns. As a more thoughtful response than I was able to muster yesterday, let me first say aloud some things we already know.

You appear to be responding not only to a present situation but also to a remembrance of pain in the past, which the "new" triggers. This is certainly to be expected but must be verbalized to help us keep perspective. I will keep praying that this situation has a more positive outcome and that someone lends support and encouragement.

The church is not a pastor, a few insulated folks; the church is far more than you and I could ever dream or hope. The church is in the world, the tendrils of a mighty vine that have slow but mighty power. The power comes not from the number of tendrils but from the root from the Spirit rising through all. Though tendrils would like the help of other shoots and branches, they may work alone—are called to be faithful even when it appears they are alone for they are never alone. The power is with them. You are in the world because you are called and gifted where you are. Support from others doesn't increase the importance of what you do. Lack of understanding on the part of others, unwillingness to join you in your struggle to help families and individuals achieve their potential, decency, justice, and power to a greater extent do not diminish the importance of your work. You are you; your work is your work. Their value is intrinsic, not given by others nor diminished by others' ignorance or lack of participation.

You are too wise to forget that we change institutions from the inside. We don't give up that power by walking away from something that seems crippled, ineffectual—nearly hopeless—unless we have honestly confronted the truth that God's power is limitless, and we have still lost hope. Given the overwhelming demands on you and your deep desire to make a difference in people's lives, you are too wise not to ask. Is the church the best place to use my time and gifts? Well, friend, who else would be able to witness to the folks in the pews as well as you? Don't be trapped by thinking it's a one-way missionary voyage to "out there." Christian discipleship is lifelong in and through which we witness outward and inward. You keep the huddled sheep in the fold from being totally deaf, blind, or dumb because you have been "out there"—where many of them should also be. You return to the "country of the Blind" and offer them new vision because you are gifted with sight.

You need to read something by a liberation theologian, I suspect. Perhaps you are feeling, too, what many today feel—that the church has lost the vision of the world. Others just think the church is too outdated in methods. Whatever the problems, they are not new. You know too much of church history to trivialize this problem or not to be frustrated by it—that it wasn't already solved in the last several centuries.

Now that you have carefully analyzed my questions about your sense of call and know yourself to be called to ministry as a layperson, it is time for you to claim the power promised to followers. I see in you some self-defeating behaviors—or what may be taken by others who know you less well than I as such. Sometimes you look, sit, move, stand, speak, and laugh as if you expect your mother's judgment to be what you receive in response to your offerings. What of your father's more objective and valuable judgment? Will you not receive that? Will you not accept that? I hear people speak of how "brilliant" you are. I respect that mind. I also respect your vision and judgment. I'd like you to claim your authority. You are called by God and gifted by God. Be the author of what you are, cocreator with the Author. Don't short-circuit what may yet be self-doubt.

Only because I accept you exactly as you are in all your beauty and ordinariness and specialness do I challenge you: let it come forth not so that you may be glorified but so Christ is in or through you. And I dare mention ordinariness, because that is what God made most beautiful, sanctifying them through the incarnation and other self-revelation and ordinary human existence in its wonder, glory, or plainness. You confuse people with the mixed messages of weak or strong.

I had to invite or question you about the ordained ministry. I heard you tentatively mention more than once, "Maybe ..." I felt it was important for you to define your call and particularly now as you seem to be asking, "Where to ...?" Only because of the depth of my concern have I spoken. I know we have been blunt—I hope not once perhaps cruel. Your weariness, the constant onslaught of cases, concerns, and situations are exhausting. "The poor have always ..." I'm concerned. I know you are so giving that the boundaries would be broad, even if everyone else weren't expecting as much from you. How can we help you to be refilled, refreshed, reengaged without loading more work on you? How can we schedule what you need? I hope my deep love and concern, which motivate this letter, are somehow reaching my too-weary friend.

How, where, can we simplify? Wood-carving shop and bare necessities—space, time, silence—peace. Please God, let it be!

And, friend, whatever happens with Chaddock, know this from one who sees much of what is or has been happening: You have made a difference. You do make a difference. I have not ceased, and will not cease, to pray for you.

Your pastor and friend,
Mary

I'm off to see the bishop! If you are still speaking to me, I'd love to hear from you on Saturday.*

* Mary wrote this letter to me (Sidney) on September 28,1989.

I hope you have been blessed by the journey through some of the writings of Rev. Mary Vick Roth.

—Sidney L. Brackman Crowcroft

Endnotes

1   Henri J. Nouwin, *The Wounded Healer: Ministry in Contemporary Society* (New York: Doubleday, 1979).

2   Eugene H. Peterson, *A Long Obedience in the Same Direction: Discipleship in an Instant Society* (Downers Grove, Illinois: InterVarsity Press, 1980).

3   Henry Van Dyke, *The Story of the Other Wiseman* (Brewster, Massachusetts: Paraclete Press, 1984).

4   Annie Dillard, *Teaching Stones to Talk: Expectations and Encounters* (New York: Harper and Rowe, 1982), 31.

5   Gertrude Mueller Nelson, *To Dance with God: Family Rituals and Community* Celebrations (Mahway, New Jersey: Paulist Press, 1986), 3.

6   Claudia Bepko and JoAnn Krestan, *Too Good for Her Own Good: Breaking Free from the Burden of Female Responsibility* (New York: Harper and Rowe, 1990).

7   Karen Payne, ed., *Between Ourselves: Letters between Mothers and Daughters, 1750-1982* (Boston: Houghton-Mifflin, 1983), 3-4.

About the Author

Because of her mother's death when she was two years old, Mary was raised by her aunt and uncle who reluctantly allowed her to live with them and their children. The love of God was shown to her through weekend visits with her grandmother. It was her grandmother's love and learning to read at an early age that stimulated her imagination and saved her from becoming a bitter adult. She married at an early age (18) to at last have the family she had dreamed of as a child.

She earned a bachelor's degree in English and education, a master's degree in counseling, and a specialist endorsement all from Eastern Illinois University. She earned a Master of Divinity degree from Garrett-Evangelical Theological Seminary . She was voted the best preacher in her seminary class and became the first woman to serve a full term as a District Superintendent in the Illinois Great Rivers Conference of the United Methodist Church (formerly the Central and Southern Illinois Conferences).